ADVANCE PRAISE FOR

Navigating Moments of Hesitation: Portraits of Evangelical English Language Arts Teachers

"*Navigating Moments of Hesitation* takes a close look at a largely unexplored and often taboo aspect of K-12 education: how teachers' religious beliefs influence their classroom instruction. In this book, Hadley provides detailed portraits of three evangelical Christian teachers and offers a critical analysis of the role religion plays in how these teachers enact their formal instruction and engage with students who have aspects of their identities that contradict Biblical teachings. Although the portraits are of language arts teachers, this book offers important insights for practitioners and teacher educators in all subject areas."

Wayne Journell
Professor and Associate Chair
Teacher Education and Higher Education
University of North Carolina at Greensboro

"In this remarkable book, Dr. Hadley focuses on a group of educators who receive little attention from scholars, but whom many of us will recognize from our work in schools: Christian teachers who try to serve both their most foundational core beliefs and also the needs of their students in a rapidly-changing world. Hadley's sensitive account will be of great value in education classes to help people explore their own developing identities as teachers. She has a great talent for writing, for rigorous analysis and for making complex ideas accessible but, most of all, this book is grounded in her voice and her story as an educator and a woman who has navigated a similar journey in her own life. A deeply insightful, honest and readable book."

Julian Edgoose
Former Associate/Research Professor
University of Puget Sound

"This timely book explores critically important paradoxes about evangelicalism, teacher education, and inclusion in US public school English classrooms. A Derridean lensing of hospitality and welcome leads English educator Heidi Hadley to ask profoundly difficult questions such as: "How could I model for my evangelical students what it means to accept all students into their classroom if I wasn't willing to accept their religious identity in my classroom? But if I did unconditionally accept their religious identity and welcome their religious ways of knowing and being—which includes, of course, religiously informed transphobia and homophobia—into my teacher education classroom, would they turn around and create classrooms that excluded LGBTQ+ students?" This study offers no easy answers; instead, it offers compelling, sympathetic interpretations of how a researcher and three early-career teachers honestly and inventively grappled with the various ways (Christian) religious identities can make English teacher identities possible."

Mary M. Juzwik, Professor
Departments of Teacher Education and English
Michigan State University

"Hadley takes readers by the hand and guides them through the ways in which religion can directly and indirectly inform educators' moves in the English Language Arts classroom. Although Hadley's study focuses on Christian teachers, the implications of her research are far-reaching and support the cultivation of a pluralistic society."

Denise Dávila, Assistant Professor
Department of Curriculum and Instruction
University of Texas Austin

Navigating Moments of Hesitation

Critical Perspectives on Religion and Education

Kevin Burke and Avner Segall, *Editors*

Recent work in resacralization and postsecularism takes the stance that public education is always and already religious education not only because of the historical remnants that persist in and around the educational project or because education is inherently a missionary endeavor, but also in the bodies and minds that enter schools on a daily basis, carrying with them strains of religious sentiment and experience that can't help but shape a schooled life. The same applies to many of school's procedures and vocabulary. The series is interested in studies that take seriously the ways in which religion shapes the educational experience and is equally concerned with thinking back through certain religious languages, discourses and practices that might make new kinds of critiques of the educational project differently possible. The question, then, isn't if religion is present in and relevant to education but how its relevance can be better understood, reworked, potentially challenged or fruitfully reinforced.

Books in the Series

Navigating Moments of Hesitation:
Portraits of Evangelical English Language Arts Teachers
by Heidi Lyn Hadley (2021)

If you have a project that you wish to have considered for publication, please send a proposal, one or two sample chapters, and your current CV to: Kevin Burke (burkekq@gmail.com) or Avner Segall (avner@msu.edu).

Navigating Moments of Hesitation

Portraits of Evangelical English Language Arts Teachers

By Heidi Lyn Hadley

GORHAM, MAINE

Published by Myers Education Press, LLC
P.O. Box 424 Gorham, ME 04038

Myers Education Press is an academic publisher specializing in books, e-books, and digital content in the field of education. All of our books are subjected to a rigorous peer review process and produced in compliance with the standards of the Council on Library and Information Resources.

Library of Congress Cataloging-in-Publication Data available from Library of Congress.

13-digit ISBN 978-1-9755-0363-5 (paperback)
13-digit ISBN 978-1-9755-0362-8 (hard cover)
13-digit ISBN 978-1-9755-0364-2 (library networkable e-edition)
13-digit ISBN 978-1-9755-0365-9 (consumer e-edition)

Printed in the United States of America.

All first editions printed on acid-free paper that meets the American National Standards Institute Z39-48 standard.

Cover design by Teresa Lagrange.

CONTENTS

ACKNOWLEDGMENTS

THIS BOOK WOULD NOT be possible without the support of Kevin J. Burke, who read this manuscript early and often and always asked the questions that helped me discover what it was I was really trying to say. I have learned a great deal about hospitality, generosity, and research from him, particularly in the way he made space and held space for me in research projects and in research spaces. I also owe a great deal to Hilary E. Hughes and Jennifer M. Graff, who helped make this study better and offered criticism in the kindest ways possible. Their incisive comments and insightful suggestions were deeply appreciated. I would be remiss if I do not acknowledge the contributions of the many colleagues and scholars in the Language and Literacy Education department at the University of Georgia who mentored me as a researcher and as a teacher educator during my years there.

Thanks, too, to the three exceptional teachers—Mallory, Mei, and Noelle—who opened their classrooms to me, answered my very personal religious questions with so much grace, and trusted me with their stories.

As always, thanks to my five delightfully feral children (Ivy, Spencer, Jacob, Logan, and Caleb) and my very responsible partner, Rhett, who all generously took care of each other or fended for themselves when I needed space and time to read, think, and write.

PART I

Framing the Portraits

I WAS RAISED A Mormon,[1] which seems like a fairly straightforward statement of fact. It might be more accurate to say I was born a Mormon because my parents' temple marriage doctrinally meant I was "born in the covenant." However it's said, it would be hard to overestimate the vast reach and scope of Mormonism's influence on my life—as a young person, as a teacher, as a researcher, and as a mother. Basically, you could take any identity or persona that I've taken on in my life and I could tell you in five sentences or fewer how Mormonism or a reaction to Mormonism has shaped that identity. For me, as a child and as a teen, Mormonism made a lot of things possible: My seven siblings and I were the direct result of the Mormon interpretation of the charge to "go forth, multiply, and replenish the earth" (Genesis 1:28, King James Version), but Mormonism also served as the regulatory discourse that makes parenting a large family possible. As a relatively obedient Mormon teenager, I didn't smoke. I didn't drink. I didn't do drugs. I didn't have sex. I felt bad for making out (a simulation of the sex act!). I didn't watch R-rated movies (and my parents were not that happy about PG-13 movies either). Things I did do: read the scriptures, pray twice (or more!) a day, attend early morning seminary (basically, an extra class held at the church across from my high school during which we studied the scriptures), serve as the vice president of the seminary council, go to church every Sunday, go to youth group every Wednesday, work on my goals for my Personal Progress award (the female equivalent of the Eagle Scout award that the boys completed), and attend the Mormon temple every few months to perform baptisms for the dead.[2] Although my upbringing might seem restrictive to some, I had a happy childhood. Following the teachings of Mormonism, my parents were (and are) kind and, while they had high expectations for us, our home was also a place of laughter, family dinners, and creative play.

My parents also valued children as human beings who deserved respect even while they were in the process of learning and growing.

As I moved into young adulthood, it seemed natural to attend the church's flagship university, Brigham Young University in Provo, Utah. In the middle of my studies, I served a year-and-a-half-long mission proselytizing in Birmingham, England. I came back home, already too old to still be a single woman by Mormon standards of the time (I was 22). By my 23rd birthday, I had finished my last year of college, gotten engaged, graduated, gotten married, and started teaching high school English in a small town outside of Provo while my husband finished his degree.

Mormonism influenced my adult decisions, too: My desire to have a large family was largely influenced by Mormon family values; my decision to quit teaching after the birth of my second child was a direct result of the Mormon prophets' counseling that families should ideally have a stay-at-home mother. We moved for my husband's career—first Texas, then Alabama, and then Georgia—and I had babies all along the way. My children, too, were born into the covenant because my husband and I had been married in the temple. All of this to say, for me, Mormonism was and is both a religion and an identity. Mormonism constructed me and allowed me to construct myself over and over and over again in new states, as a mother, as a teacher, as a wife, and as a woman.

It might be enough to simply say that I'm not sure when the *break* happened—when I suddenly realized that I had doubts and that I was so tired of doing the endless mental gymnastics that allowed me to make sense of the casual misogyny, homophobia, and racism of the church's policies and doctrines. It might have started from the moment I picked up my first book as a child and entered worlds where other thoughts were thinkable, where other ways of being were possible—certainly my parents saw the danger in books; even while they encouraged me to read the best books, they also threw away books that didn't meet their approval (read: had sex in them). It might have started during my mission in England, where I felt more like a cog in a corporate machine than a spiritual minister to humanity. Certainly, the easiest story to tell is that it started when my favorite brother came out and identified himself as gay—an identity that the church (at the time, at least) had said was less about identity and more about apostasy.[3] My love and respect for my brother opened the possibility of attending to new-to-me ways of thinking about gender and sexuality with a complexity that had been previously impossible. The "official" break happened some 10 years later, when the church's position on the baptism of children with gay parents was leaked in the media—a position so homophobic and punitive as to make my decision to not attend church relatively easy.

But a *break* is never really a break. Yes, I no longer attend the Mormon Church. Mormonism is an important part of who I have been, but it is still a part of what has made me who I am and who I am becoming. I still consider myself to be a heritage Mormon—which for me means that I acknowledge the deep role Mormonism plays in my heritage, my family, my culture, and my sense of who I am and might be while rejecting the religious doctrines, beliefs, and truth claims of the religion itself. There are weird, filamental leftovers of practice—coffee still smells like sin to me,[4] for example, and I still can't wear sleeveless shirts without feeling a little tawdry. Most important, for this study of evangelical Christian teachers, my heritage Mormon identity has left me with an understanding of the pervasive and fundamental influence of religion on every aspect of my life. My religious identity and the religious discourse I was surrounded by certainly shaped what version of teacherhood I performed as a high school teacher.

I applied for graduate school almost simultaneously with my final *break* from Mormonism. I remember speaking with my soon-to-be advisor about his research interests, and he mentioned that he studied religion and education—a topic, it seemed to me, that was personally interesting but not actually connected to real work, real teachers, or real kids. I enrolled in his graduate seminar on religion and teaching, partly because it felt like I should—what with power dynamics being what they are in academia—but also out of curiosity. Was it really possible to build a reputable career out of a personal interest on an even more personal topic like religion? Shouldn't I focus my time on things like reading fluency or effective writing instruction? My enrollment in the class coincided with my first assignment to teach preservice teachers, and the combination of the two experiences was eye-opening. First, I learned from the seminar readings that people *were* doing real work about religion with real teachers and real kids from a variety of perspectives. There were studies that looked at the different literacy practice of high schoolers from different religions (Rackley, 2014) and scholars who argued for the inclusion of religious topics in curriculum and teacher education programs as a way of building a diverse, pluralistic society (James, 2015; Kunzman, 2006; Nord & Haynes, 1998). There were books that traced the often-contested boundaries and relationship of religion and education through U.S. history (DelFattore, 2004).

At the same time I was learning about the real work being done by educational researchers on the topic of religion and education in my course work, I was working with my first group of preservice teachers in Teaching Writing to Adolescents. These preservice teachers were bright, engaged, nervous, *and* excited about teaching. Through a final project for my religion course—and in conjunction with a fellow graduate student, William Fassbender—I interviewed several of these preservice teachers about the way religion influenced their concepts of teaching, their experience in our preservice teaching program, and their beliefs about students. In these interviews, William and I found that many of our evangelical Christian students directly connected their teaching to a sense of "calling" and felt silenced or othered in their education courses, particularly in discussions that centered on social justice or LGBTQ+-supportive classroom practices. Furthermore, some of them were actively (but privately) grappling with their role as an evangelical Christian in a public school classroom (Hadley & Fassbender, 2020). That first project led to a continued interest in the religious lives of teachers (including my own). In subsequent years, after William and I completed our initial study, I continued interviewing evangelical Christian preservice teachers about their religion, their beliefs about teaching, and their experiences in the teacher preparation program. As a result of these interviews, I often wondered how these teachers made sense of their religious calling to teach with the actual demands of public school teaching. This book, then, is a response to that wondering.

I share all this about my own religious and educational background to make clear my own positionality and interest in the topic of religion, evangelical Christian teachers, and education. As a result of my experiences, I approach this research as a formerly devoutly religious person who also carries a certain amount of anger and skepticism toward the religion of my childhood and, more broadly, religion in general. One of the discursive moves that was made in my church to quell skepticism was to say, "The church is perfect; people aren't."[5] A practicing Mormon friend of mine put it more plainly: "I hate Mormons, but I love the doctrines of the Mormon

Church." My own stance toward religion might be best stated as the complete opposite: I admire and respect religious people, but I have a great deal of skepticism toward religions themselves, particularly as religion relates to issues of power, equity, and justice.

What this means for this portraiture study of evangelical Christian teachers is that the reader should attend to my positionality as a portraitist as closely as they do to the portraits themselves—particularly the ways in which my affection for and affinity with evangelical Christian teachers and my ambivalence about the general religious project color my analysis and representation. In art and in research, every portrait is as much a portrait of the portraitist as it is of the portrait's subject (Bloom & Erlandson, 2005). I don't think it is possible, per se, for an accounting of my own positionality to erase the ways that my experiences guide my analysis and representations of the data I collected, but I do wish to make my positionality and relevant experiences clear for readers.

Notes

1. The Mormon Church is officially titled the Church of Jesus Christ of Latter-day Saints. I continue to refer to it as "Mormon" despite the fact that the current prophet has asked members to use the full title. Some of this is nostalgic—we called ourselves Mormons for my entire childhood and young adult life, and I feel uncomfortable using any other term. But some of it is also a personal choice to resist what I see as a rebranding movement meant to obscure from the public less favorable associations with Mormonism and Mormons.

2. Because Mormons believe that baptism is necessary for entrance into the kingdom of heaven, baptisms for the dead (or baptism of a living person as a proxy for a dead person) are performed by faithful members in Mormon temples. Mormon youth can serve as proxy beginning at age 12.

3. In the Mormon Church, the term *apostasy* or *apostate* can be applied to any church member who disagrees with church leaders or church doctrine, but it has generally been reserved for serious issues of difference that involve encouraging other people to leave the church as well. In recent years, it had most frequently been used as a label for members who were actively leading other members astray—especially in terms of modern polygamous practice or an attempt to establish a separate church. Apostasy can lead to excommunication from the church, which still happens regularly within the Mormon Church. The term also is used—generally in a half-joking way—to refer to anyone who has left the church or who doesn't follow the guidance of the church in terms of dietary restrictions, sexual practice, and so on.

4. This is especially ironic considering that, in theory at least, I no longer believe in the general concept of sin.

5. In recent years, I have noticed a shift in this discursive move to "The doctrine is perfect; the church isn't." This coincided with moves within the church to be more transparent about the racist history of the church.

References

Bloom, C. M., & Erlandson, D. A. (2003). Three voices in portraiture: Actor, artist, and audience. *Qualitative Inquiry, 9*(6), 874–894.

DelFattore, J. (2004). *The fourth R: Conflicts over religion in America's public schools.* Yale University Press.

Hadley, H. L., & Fassbender, W. J. (2020). Recognizing religious identity in preservice teachers. In M. Juzwik, D. Davila, J. Stone, & K. Burke (Eds.), *Christian religious literacies: Histories, implications and alternative readings* (pp. 37–50). Routledge.

James, J. H. (2015). Toward democratic living and learning. In J. H. James (Ed.), *Religion in the classroom: Dilemmas for democratic education* (pp. 5–12). Routledge.

Kunzman, R. (2006). *Grappling with the good: Talking about religion and morality in public schools.* State University of New York Press.

Nord, W. A., & Haynes, C. C. (1998). *Taking religion seriously across the curriculum.* Association for Supervision and Curriculum Development.

Rackley, E. D. (2014). Scripture based discourses of Latter-day Saint and Methodist youths. *Reading Research Quarterly, 49*(4), 417–435.

CHAPTER ONE

Christian Teachers, Public Schools, and the Impossibility of Neutrality

Religion and education in the United States have long had a complex relationship. Almost from the beginning of publicly funded education in the United States, conflict over *how* religion might be taught in public education erupted. At first, it was a question not of whether the Bible would be taught but, instead, over *whose* (Catholic or Protestant) Bible would be taught. As the United States became a more pluralistic society, the very imbrication of religion and education began to be questioned (DelFattore, 2004). Despite numerous court cases that attempt to clarify the role that public education (and funding) can play in religious instruction and expression (e.g., *Abington School District v. Schempp*, 1963; *Lemon v. Kurtzman*, 1971), the U.S. educational system continues to be intertwined in Christian practice and belief, from the school calendar to the languaging of teacher/student relationships to the bell schedules that separate periods of study and learning (Burke & Segall, 2015).

Even today, it is not uncommon for courts to rule on whether a kindergartner in California violated the constitutional separation between church and state by handing out candy canes with a poem about the birth of Christ (Landau, 2014), whether districts that implement yoga as part of a physical education curriculum are favoring certain religions over others (Calvert, 2013), or whether a Washington state high school coach can kneel and engage in prayer with players after a game (Stempel, 2017). The American Civil Liberties Union recently filed a suit against a Louisiana school district where evangelical bulletin boards, evolution-denouncing guest speakers, and student readings of the Lord's Prayer during class time are commonplace (Weaver, 2017). These kinds of legal brangles over how much or how little religion is acceptable in publicly funded education indicate the continuing interest and divide in the intertwining of religion and education in the United States.

Current research on religious teachers makes it clear that teachers' religious identities do influence the way that they navigate classroom spaces. I include here studies that attend to K–12 public school teachers, although this study specifically examines secondary teachers because the research that has been done on the religious identities and teacher practice of religious teachers has been quite small. Previous research established that teachers are more religious than the American public at large (Slater, 2000), that many religious teachers pray about their jobs and their students (Hartwick, 2015a, 2015b), and that religious beliefs and practices influence *how* teachers behave in classrooms (Huerta & Flemmer, 2005; Journell, 2011; White, 2010). Additional research underscores the general unpreparedness of preservice teachers to teach from multiple religious perspectives (Anderson et al., 2015; Bruce & Bailey, 2014; Marks et al., 2014; Subedi, 2006). What is missing from the currently available research on teachers is research that examines how teachers are making sense of their own experiences as a religious person in a public school classroom. Furthermore, there is a need for research that examines how religious teachers are navigating complicated ethical issues within their classrooms, particularly because there is an assumption of religious neutrality in these spaces (Nord & Haynes, 1998)—current research on teachers' religious identities, including this book, challenges assumptions of neutrality as likely being an impossibility.

Purpose of the Study

At its broadest, this study explores the experiences of evangelical Christian teachers in the Deep South to flesh out more fully (beyond surveys and short-answer questions) the tensions experienced by Christian evangelical teachers in public school classrooms. As White (2009) pointed out in her study of the connection of teachers' religious beliefs with their classroom practice, "how teachers use their own religious beliefs to navigate . . . [classroom] decisions is silenced" (p. 859). With so little research focusing on how Christian evangelical teachers build a teacher identity that bridges their religious beliefs and their educational philosophy, this study more narrowly aims to explore how new teachers (those with 3 years or less in the classroom) are navigating tensions between their personal religious and spiritual beliefs and the role of a teacher in an increasingly diverse, pluralistic, and cosmopolitan public school system. Initial interviews from a pilot study (Hadley & Fassbender, 2019) indicated that for these teachers, there is a great deal of uncertainty as to how they might approach issues of gender, sex, sexuality, and power in classroom interactions with students, which this study confirms. However, this study also highlights other issues of classroom practice that evangelical Christian teachers feel unsure about. This study attempts to understand what three evangelical Christian new teachers *do* with that uncertainty and tension.

Study Considerations

The overarching goal of this book is to present honest, complex, and complicating portraits of evangelical Christian teachers as they navigate the first few years of teaching in a public school setting. One of my concerns as a researcher and author centers on my own ethical orientation to my participants. In educational research, religion is often either ignored or positioned as a problem; religious teachers are often positioned as stupid or mean-spirited (more on this in the literature review). My own previous research with religious preservice teachers showed me how easy it would be to simply pull the most shocking statements the participants make (shocking, of course, to a liberal, religiously skeptical audience) and string them together in an excoriation of religion and religious teachers in general. Such an approach would, at the very least, miss the complexity of the participants and risk oversimplifying a complicated experience.

As a result of these concerns, I chose to frame this study using Derridean deconstruction of the concepts of ethics and hospitality—a framework that relies on poststructural understandings of discourse, which allows me to position and understand my participants as products and producers of discourse (more on this in the theoretical framework section). I also chose to use portraiture as the guiding methodology for my study, in no small part because portraiture *insists* that the researcher looks for *goodness* in research sites and participants, and attempts to account for what the definition of goodness is for the participants themselves. Because evangelical teachers report feeling othered within the larger educational discourse (Ahn et al., 2016; Hadley & Fassbender, 2019), I attempt here to attend closely to my own ethical responsibility to study participants by considering how I offer hospitality to them throughout the study.

Definition of Terms

Religion

I use both *faith* and *religion* to describe the social practices and belief systems shared by the participants in this study. A precise, broad definition of *religion* itself is still proving to be somewhat linguistically slippery, although there are several workable definitions. Early sociological work (Durkheim, 1915/1965) defined religion as a codified system that distinguishes between the sacred and profane, more recent sociological work defines it as a "stable cluster of values, norms, statuses, roles, and groups developed around a basic social need" (Smith, 1995, p. 905). Other definitions of religion focus on beliefs in supernatural events or superhuman beings (Smith, 1995). Religious scholars (Nash, 2001; Newman, 2004) distinguish spirituality as an inward expression of personal faith (a term with another slippery meaning but most easily understood as trust in or loyalty to a concept of being), whereas religion is defined as an outward expression of that faith.

Although I have attempted to specify between religion, in general (which includes multiple belief systems with wide and varied belief and worship systems), and Christianity, specifically, other scholars who have done work around religion in education in the United States often use the terms as vaguely interchangeable, a usage that attests to the dominant role that Christianity has played in the United States at large. In these instances, I have attempted to draw distinctions where possible. I use the term *religious teachers* when that term is used by other educational scholars, but in these cases, unless specified, the term can be understood to have strong connections (but perhaps not exclusionary connections) with Christianity. For example, a study might report the results of a survey of "religious teachers" and Christian participants might make up 90% of the studied religious teachers. Although technically the study includes data and responses from teachers who do not identify as Christian, the findings of the study are overwhelmingly influenced by Christianity. For this study, I refer to the participants as "evangelical Christian teachers" or "evangelical teachers" to specify which religion I am specifically referencing. I do, however, refer to the participants' "religious beliefs," and this should be read as a direct reference to their Christian religious beliefs.

Evangelical Christians

The selected participants of this study all identify as evangelical Christians—a term that encompasses a wide variety of Christian faith traditions. *Evangelical Christianity* is a term that "crosses denominational, racial, political, and numerous other boundaries" (Juzwik, 2014, p. 336) and includes groups such as White Southern Baptists, Latin American Pentecostals, Anabaptists, and predominantly Black Bible-believing churches (Juzwik, 2014). However, evangelicals are tied together by certain common beliefs (sometimes called "closed doctrines"). Evangelical Christians are distinguished by a belief in the Bible as an authoritative text, a personal relationship with Jesus Christ, and a belief that salvation comes through His grace. Furthermore, evangelicals have an understanding of their own personal responsibility to exert a redemptive influence on culture, politics, and sociocultural discourses (Juzwik, 2014).

This definition of evangelical Christianity can be complicated because evangelicals can be closely aligned with fundamental Christian movements (among others). For example, one of the participants of the study personally attends an evangelical nondenominational church but attended a private fundamentalist Christian school (fundamentalism differs from evangelism in that fundamentalists believe in a separation of themselves from the world as a means of attaining doctrinal purity). Furthermore, none of the participants in this study attended highly charismatic churches (which tend to be more common among Pentecostal evangelicals). Charismatic churches and congregations experience worship that prioritizes a showing forth of the gifts of the Spirit (faith healings, speaking in tongues, etc.), and although the participants were quick to assure me that they did believe in the gifts of the Spirit, they didn't feel spiritual gifts should be the center of the worship experience.

New Teachers

I purposefully have chosen to focus my study on new teachers, who I define as teachers in their first 3 years of teaching. Ease of access to participants matters here—I have been teaching preservice teachers for 4 years now, and these are teachers with whom I have strong relationships of trust, a bond that ideally allows us to discuss matters of faith and teaching with a certain amount of openness. But I also have a very specific reason for working with new teachers: I am interested in studying them in the act of early-career identity formation, while they are still teaching in tentative and sometimes uneasy starts, conscious of many of the choices and ethical moments that many experienced teachers have already automated through years of practice.

Although this research on new teachers has implications for teacher induction programs, improving teacher induction programs is not the primary focus of this study. What this study might do is point out some of the ways that teacher identity (and particularly religious teachers' identity) has been largely ignored as an important component of supporting new teachers within teacher induction programs. Teacher induction programs have traditionally been created to address high attrition rates among teachers. Studies have shown that just below half of teachers leave the profession during their first 5 years of teaching (Grissmer & Kirby, 1987; Ingersoll, 2003; Ingersoll & May, 2011). Teacher induction programs have typically focused on supporting teachers by attending to issues such as socialization, adjustment, professional development, and assessment (Ingersoll & Strong, 2011), and this support has often taken the form of mentoring programs (Britton et al., 2003; Hobson et al., 2009). This study of evangelical new teachers also illuminates some of the challenges of new teachers not previously accounted for within teacher induction programs.

Religious Identity

I use the term *religious identity* as a shorthand term to describe the beliefs and practices of the participants, but my use of the term *identity* is tentative. Like Butler (2004, p. 121), I remain (and hope to remain) "permanently troubled by identity categories" that essentialize, reduce, and simplify. When I use the term *religious identity*, it should be understood as an acknowledgment of the deconstruction of the concept of identity that Derrida encourages through the concept of différance—the difference that "shatters the cult of identity and the dominance of Self or Other" (Guillemette & Cossette, 2006, p. 3) and keeps the Self from being identical to itself. Although I follow Derrida's lead in using the term *identity*, I do acknowledge that much of my conception of "identity" is influenced by poststructural conceptions of the subject, subjectivity, and identity. When Derrida speaks of deconstructing the subject, he does not intend to destroy the subject or delegitimize the subject. Instead, he explains that "when you deconstruct the subject, you analyze all the hidden assumptions which are implied in the philosophical, or the ethical, or the juridical, or the political use of the concept of 'subject'" (Derrida, 2001, p. 178). Derrida views deconstruction of the subject not as an act of obliteration, but as an act of questioning with the view to "*improve* the concept of the human subject" (2001, p. 179), particularly when historical configurations of subjecthood have precluded women, children, and non-Europeans (among many other formal identities), from being considered subjects.

This is not to say that Derrida dismisses the concept of identity or is dismissive of identity politics (for my purposes, this is important as religious identity is an important piece of my study). Rather, Derrida invites a more complicated conception of identity, one that attends to alterity and works against societal and cultural constructs that insist on homogeneity at the expense of the other—a stance that is particularly helpful as I consider the identity construction and subjectivity of the teachers and classrooms I research. Derrida is suspicious, however, of any identity construction that defines identity as exclusive or homogenizing:

> People who fight for their identity must pay attention to the fact that identity is not the self-identity of a thing, but implies a difference within identity. That is, the identity of a culture is a way of being different from itself . . . language is different from itself; the person is different from itself. Once you take into account this inner and other difference, then you pay attention to the other and you understand that fighting for your own identity is not exclusive of another identity, is open to another identity. And this prevents totalitarianism, nationalism, egocentrism, and so on. (Derrida, 1997, p. 13)

While this attention to difference within identity is important, of particular use to my study is how Derrida frames the interiority or the individuality of identity as open to possibility as well. It is not enough for a person to attend only to the otherness of other persons, but deconstruction opens the person themselves to be "open to another identity"—to attend to (and welcome in) both interior and exterior alterity. Because I want to look at how teachers navigate their own identity formations, this conception of the deconstructed subject as being open to another identity and inner alterity seems especially pertinent.

Religion and Education: Current Understandings and Framings

Educational theorists and practitioners have begun to grapple with what it might mean to "take religion seriously" (Nord & Haynes, 1998) in educational spaces. There are numerous conceptual articles or books that have added to the overall discussion of why or how religion might be conceptualized and taught within American public school classrooms (most notably, Burke & Segall, 2017; Carper & Hunt, 2011; Haynes, 2012; James, 2015; Kunzman, 2006; Nord, 2010; Nord & Haynes, 1998; Rogers, 2011; Waggoner, 2016).

In their influential book *Taking Religion Seriously Across the Curriculum*, Nord and Haynes (1998) lay out an argument that religion can and should be taught in all public schools and in every content area. They argue that religion has a place in public schools in the United States for both civic and educational reasons. From a civic standpoint, they argue that American conceptions of liberty are "built on the conviction that it is possible to find common ground in spite of . . . deep religious differences" (Nord & Hayes, 1998, p. 8) What this might mean for educators is that although they may not agree with the religious beliefs and practices of students in their classroom, these beliefs and practices must not be excluded from the discourse of public education. Nord and Haynes argue that moves in the 20th century to exclude religion from public school curricula were unjust because "it means that we don't take religious people seriously" (1998, p. 8). For Nord and Haynes, the exclusion of religious discussion in American classrooms is a violation of the neutrality required of public schools by the First Amendment.

From an educational standpoint, Nord and Haynes (1998) also see educational reasons for engaging seriously with religion across content and subject areas. They argue that engaging seriously with religion and religious ideas is an imperative part of a truly liberal education because religion has influenced the way that humans make sense of the world around them. For

Nord and Haynes, "there are both secular *and* religious ways of asking, reflecting on, and answering . . . unavoidable 'existential questions'" (1998, p. 38). An education that is devoid of a serious exploration of the ways that religious traditions have answered these questions—or just as problematically for Nord and Haynes, an education that places religion's relevance to these questions in the distant past—ignores what Nord and Haynes believe are the underpinnings of a balanced liberal education.

Educational scholars in the United States continue to build on initial work by Nord and Haynes (1998) by putting forward their own ideas about how the religiosity of students, teachers, and American society at large might be "taken seriously." Carper and Hunt (2011), two self-described religious conservative educational researchers, argue that Nord and Haynes do not go far enough to adequately address the rights of religious families to educate their children within their own faith traditions. They call, instead, for a "disestablishing" (Carper & Hunt, 2011, p. 82) of public education in favor of a model of education that privileges parental rights to educate children according to their own beliefs. What this might look like in terms of school policy today, of course, would mean vouchers for religious private schools and loosely regulated homeschool options.

A very common frame used to argue for the study of religious teachers is the framework of multicultural studies, referencing the work of Ladson-Billings (1994, 2000) and Nieto (1996). This framing positions both teachers' religions and the religions of their students as an identity category—an identity category that often overlaps with linguistic, ethnic, and racial diversity. In these studies (Dedeoglu & Lamme, 2011; Huerta & Flemmer, 2005; Juzwik & McKenzie, 2015), the need to understand teachers' religious identities is centered in the argument that teachers must understand religious identities (their own and others') to effectively connect with diverse student populations, create a curriculum that includes multiple and diverse perspectives and experiences, and, by extension, teach students to appreciate multiple and diverse perspectives and experiences—all without having to relinquish their own beliefs and religious identity. A critique of this kind of approach to religious teachers might be that the student is always positioned as the other of the teacher, and the teacher is positioned as the norm of the classroom. Situating teachers' religious beliefs and religious understandings as only important in cases in which the majority of the students' religious identities may be different from the teachers' religious identity, may minimize the scope of religious identity on teacher practice. In fact, certain teacher practices are influenced and made possible by teachers' religious identities and beliefs regardless of whether the students in front of them share those beliefs. What might be different, of course, in situations where the teacher's religious identity is different from a student's (or a group of students') identity is that the teacher's religiously influenced practice simply becomes more visible when contrasted with the student's equally religiously influenced practice.

Other scholars, like Burke and Segall (2017), trace the ways that Christianity is already embedded in schools and schooling as a pervasive discursive figuration. For Burke and Segall, public schools in the United States are steeped in Christian metaphors and languaging, Christian-influenced calendars and schedules, and Christian-informed conceptions of kids, teachers, and education. Christian discursive figurations are always and already embedded in the very concept of what it means to teach or be a teacher through a "hidden curriculum of teaching that positions teachers as versions of Christ" (Burke & Segall, 2017, p. 13). Teachers are positioned as both martyrs—endlessly giving of their own time and money for the benefit of students until they burn out of the profession—and as saviors—entering classrooms with the intent of rescuing students from themselves, their families, their culture, and their communities. This is especially important for the participants of this study as they discuss how they navigate their classroom and student relationships as Christian teachers who are conscious of their call to perform a version of teaching that centers Christian ideals of teaching by showing forth God's love to their students.

By arguing that religion—and important for this study, Christianity—is already embedded in the discursive figurations of schools and classrooms, Burke and Segall's (2017) work can be viewed as an invitation for fellow educators and educational researchers to reframe current arguments about religion and education (which often focus on how much religion in public schools is too much or too little) to a deeper and more critical conversation about the predominantly Christian religious discourse that already exists in public school systems.

This study of evangelical Christian teachers and how their Christian identities make certain pedagogical stances and practices possible assumes that Christianity and Christian values and practices already are present and circulate within public school classrooms. Whereas Burke and Segall (2017) situate their work in a conceptual religious reading of the general practices of and assumptions *implicit* in education, teaching, and teachers, this study "takes religion seriously" by exploring how teachers' navigate their *explicit* religious identity and positionality as evangelical Christians within classrooms. Like Burke and Segall, I argue that the questions researchers ask regarding how much religion is or isn't present in classrooms or how much should be present as part of a public, taxpayer-funded education become moot because Christianity is already imbricated within public classrooms. In this study, I examine the ways that Christianity might be present in public classrooms in the beliefs and practices of evangelical teachers. Instead, what we as educational researchers might ask is how we attend to the religious tensions that are inherent in a public school system purported to be religiously neutral and pluralistic at the very same time it privileges Christianity. These tensions, of course, are already being plumbed with other identity categories like race, sexuality, gender, and class—religion has been referred to as "the last taboo subject" (Campbell & Crowe, 2015, p. xiii). What I argue here, then, is not that evangelical Christian teachers are wholly problematic or wholly unproblematic but, rather, that evangelical Christian teachers are complicated subjects who make choices about classroom ethics and practices in ways that are influenced by their religious discourses.

Although there is a growing body of research that explores what teachers believe and what they know about religion, education research that addresses *how* teachers' beliefs and religious discourses influence their teaching practice and teaching philosophy remains scant. Studies have tended to define religious literacy narrowly (largely through surveys and quantitative methods that aim to measure teachers' knowledge about world religions), and although qualitative studies do exist, the corpus of research on religion and teacher identity and practice remains very small. In the field of English education—the field in which I research and teach teacher preparation courses but, more important, the field in which the participants of this study exist—the dearth of research linking teachers' religious belief and teachers' instructional practice is even more pronounced.

Religious Teachers—Beliefs, Practices, and Identity

With the rise of identity politics and critical examinations of curriculum and public school classrooms, recent scholarship has turned to examinations of teacher identity. Increased attention to the intersections of Marxist, feminist, and critical race theories (among other critical theories) has created opportunities for scholarship that examines the positionality of teachers and how these identity markers shape their general beliefs and classroom practice (e.g., see Apple, 2013; Picower, 2009). Because teachers are overwhelmingly White, female, and middle class (National Center for Education Statistics, 2017), many scholars have focused on these identity markers as fertile ground for studies that focus on teacher identity and practice. However, teachers are also overwhelmingly religious. Slater (2008) found that teachers are more religious than other Americans (already a fairly religious group[1]) by 11 percentage points. Even accounting for gender (females, as a whole, are more likely to be religious than males), teachers still attend a place of worship regularly more than other Americans (female teachers are about 8 percentage points more likely to attend a place of worship regularly than female nonteachers; male teachers are 16 percentage points more likely to attend a place of worship regularly than male nonteachers).

While American teachers are more religious than other Americans, there has been an assumption of teacher neutrality regarding religion, that is, an assumption that teachers can hold their religious identities separate from their teacher identities. However, Slater (2008) tied teachers' religious beliefs with other trends in beliefs that are more common among teachers, particularly as compared to nonteachers with 16 or more years of education. He found that teachers were more likely than similarly educated nonteachers to have conservative views on homosexuality,[2] abortion, and pornography—stances often tied to religious beliefs. However, teachers also tend to be "more liberal than nonteachers, for example when it comes to school prayer, a stance seemingly inconsistent with their strong religious turn" (Slater, 2008, p. 51). Teachers tend to be more liberal than the general population (but not highly educated nonteachers) when it comes to issues of free speech in classroom spaces. Slater concludes that teachers "present something of a paradox" (Slater, 2008, p. 51) because they are progressive on issues like free speech and classroom prayer but seem to be more conservative on other social issues. Because Slater aggregated his data from a large national database of social science data, he was unable to definitively tie more conservative beliefs with teachers' religious identity.

In a more pointed survey study, Hartwick (2015a) directly asked Wisconsin public school K–12 teachers about their religious beliefs and how their beliefs influence their practice. Of his 317 participants, 87.9% reported that they had a belief in God, and 59% of the respondents reported that they were "called by God to teach" (Hartwick, 2015a, p. 130). Of the respondents, 50% reported that they prayed about their classroom or their students once a month or more (Hartwick, 2015b), a statistic that seems to indicate that teachers themselves are linking their professional practice with their personal religious beliefs.

Hartwick (2015a) also found a relationship between a teacher's belief in God and the kinds of classroom resources that they drew on as instructors. Teachers who professed to believe in God were "nearly twice as likely to rely solely on textbooks" (Hartwick, 2015a, p. 135) than teachers who did not believe in God. The important takeaways from these two studies, which give a broad overview of the religious beliefs of public school teachers, are, first, that public school teachers in the United States tend to be a religious, conservative group and, second, that teachers' religious beliefs may influence the decisions that they make in their classrooms.

Conversely, Hartwick's (2015b) study also suggests that the demands of the teaching profession may equally influence teachers' religious practice—including the contents of their prayers or their sense of how to fulfill the spiritual call to teach. His research suggests that teachers use prayer as a tool to help them deal with students, teachers, and administrators. Ahn and colleagues (2016) also found that evangelical Christian teachers rely on their religious beliefs to help identify and resolve moral dilemmas they face at work.

In Ahn et al.'s (2016) study, teachers and preservice teachers filled out a survey with four open-ended questions "regarding the kinds of ethical/moral dilemmas . . . participants experienced, the resources [they had available] to resolve them, and the perceived effectiveness of their teacher education programs in preparing them for dealing with their dilemma" (p. 45), and 10 closed responses that dealt with the teachers' views of how they used their faith in the resolution of moral/ethical dilemmas. Evangelical teachers who were already working in public schools reported that they had difficulty balancing their personal religious beliefs with the demands of their jobs. This included the mandate to teach tolerance to students when tolerance "goes against everything [their] religious faith teaches" (Ahn et al., 2016, p. 46). Preservice teachers reported finding unofficial Christian mentors among more experienced teachers who could give them advice about how to navigate some of the ethical issues (including pressure to change grades or how to phrase responses to students' religious questions) of being both a Christian and a teacher. Both practicing teachers and preservice teachers reported feeling underprepared by their teacher education program for these kinds of dilemmas. Ahn et al. argue that attention should be paid in teacher education programs not only to issues of cultural diversity but also to issues of spiritual and religious renewal for teachers. In short, the researchers argue that Christian students who learn about diversity and tolerance in an environment that supports (and even strengthens) their beliefs might help to ease the tensions that teachers report feeling between their personal beliefs and their professional enactment.

The obvious dilemma that these three studies highlight is twofold. First, these studies call into question not just the ability but also the desire of teachers to extract their personal religious beliefs and identity from their performance of teacher. Because so many teachers in the United States view their profession as a form of religious calling, surely it is worth asking exactly what that call entails for religious teachers. The second part of the dilemma concerns the overall concept of public education as a societal project—namely, whose conception of public education is privileged? If religious teachers view tolerance as going against everything their religious beliefs have taught them, can they support the goals of a pluralistic education for citizenship? More pointedly, perhaps, are religious teachers engaging youth to prepare them to be citizens of the pluralistic democratic republic of the United States, or are they working to prepare them to be citizens in God's kingdom? One answer here might be, as Ahn et al. (2016) argue, that engaging with teachers' religious beliefs can allow teachers to view both of these goals as parallel. For many religious teachers (including evangelical Christians), this may be true, but the participants in the researchers' study reported feeling a great deal of anxiety as they tried to prioritize *between* these two goals. Although the researchers pin this anxiety to a lack of preparation by teacher educators,[3] participant comments center the chasm between their beliefs and the demands of public school teaching practices while also acknowledging that teacher preparation did not prepare them to integrate their faith into their professional life. It seems more likely that teachers' anxiety stems from their perception of being part of two incompatible discursive figurations—the religious discourse of conversion and absolutism and the liberal educational discourse of citizenship and cosmopolitanism.

Examining Teachers' Religious Identity Outside of Discourse

While reading previous studies that examine the intersection of teacher identity and religious identity, knowledge, and practices, I found a distinct difference between studies that considered religious identity as a product of a religious discourse and studies that examined religious identities as separate from larger figurations of community, beliefs, doctrines, and practices. Researchers who centered religious teachers as part of a larger discourse—a discourse in which their beliefs and practices about teaching, youth and teachers not only *make sense* but also are, in fact, *commonsensical*—were much less likely to position individual teachers from a deficit perspective. Situating individual religious teachers as productions of discourse—productions with individual agency within the discourse, of course—creates research that presents these teachers not as ignorant zealots but as products and producers of a larger (and sometimes problematic) discourse with its own regulatory functions.

There has been a great deal of research that has been done that does not position teachers as discursive products. This research can be divided into two categories: research that gives a deficit accounting of teachers' knowledge about religion in general and research that gives a deficit accounting of teachers' personal religious identities and classroom practice.

Teacher Knowledge About Religion—The Deficit Perspective

Several studies aimed to gauge the religious literacy of preservice teachers or teachers (Anderson et al., 2015; Bruce & Bailey, 2014; Marks et al., 2014; Subedi, 2006). The American Academy of Religion (The AAR Religion in Schools Task Force, 2010) defines religious literacy as "the ability to discern and analyze the fundamental intersections of religion and social/political/cultural life through multiple lenses" (p. 4). Religiously literate teachers would have "a basic understanding of the history, central texts (where applicable), beliefs, practices and contemporary manifestations of several of the world's religious traditions" and perhaps, more important, would have "the ability to discern and explore the religious dimensions of political, social and cultural expressions across time and place" (The AAR Religion in Schools Task Force, 2010, p. 4). Although this definition of religious literacy calls for more contextualization than mere memorization of facts about religion, studies that measured religious literacy overwhelmingly conceptualized religious literacy as the amount of knowledge that teachers have about a variety of religions.

Across the board, these studies found either an inattention to religion in teacher/teacher training literature; (Bruce & Bailey, 2014) or a "lack of knowledge" (Marks et al., 2014, p. 246) about religion on the part of teachers or preservice teachers (Anderson et al., 2015; Marks et al., 2014; Subedi, 2006). Furthermore, these studies revealed that most teachers and preservice teachers feel anxiety about teaching about religion in their classrooms, even when such content is mandated by curriculum standards (Anderson et al., 2015; Subedi, 2006). With the exception of Bruce and Bailey's (2014) textual analysis, each of the studies relied heavily on quiz-like surveys to measure preservice teacher knowledge of religions, a circumstance that may explain the decontextualization of the participants from the context of their personal religious/secular discourses.

Marks and colleagues' (2014) survey study of elementary and secondary social studies preservice teachers assessed the knowledge of preservice teachers about world religions and the First Amendment religion clauses in three different university settings—a Catholic university, a rural regional campus of a larger public university, and a large public university situated in the "Bible Belt" region of the United States. The survey given consisted of 18 multiple-choice questions about a variety of world religions (e.g., "What is Ramadan?" had three possible answers: (a) The Hindu festival of lights; (b) A Jewish day of atonement; (c) The Islamic holy month). At all three institutions, researchers identified "knowledge gaps" (Marks et al., 2014, p. 253). For example, approximately 50% of the preservice teachers (across all three settings) could not identify Ramadan as the Islamic holy month (although the score at the Catholic university was higher—79% of the students answered correctly). The surveys were paired with 15 open-ended questions that also covered basic facts about religion (e.g., "Name a sacred text of Hinduism"). Data were analyzed and presented individually for each of the three schools, showing slightly higher scores of religious literacy for the preservice teachers attending the Catholic university.

This kind of survey of religious knowledge was typical of studies that attempted to measure teacher religious literacy; equally typical was the stance that researchers took to students' not knowing. In this particular study (the other survey studies were similar in this regard), preservice teachers' knowledge of religion was discussed from a deficit perspective. Language in the study (Marks et al., 2014) centered researcher dismay—one researcher wrote in the introduction to the research, "I was astounded by their lack of knowledge" (p. 246), and, later, "[I] found the severity of the students' lack of knowledge ridiculous" (p. 251). These studies all argued (and found) that preservice teachers are religiously underliterate, and although the explicit argument was to explore deficiencies in teacher preparation, implicitly, the preservice teachers themselves were framed as problematic.

Teachers' Religious Identity—The Deficit Perspective

Other articles were characterized by a conceptualization of evangelical Christian teachers' beliefs as problematic to their formation of an inclusive teaching identity. These articles, which envision the purpose of education as challenging all forms of discrimination and structural inequality, were particularly concerned with how teachers' religious beliefs might hinder their ability to enact social justice pedagogies (Blumenfeld & Jaekel, 2012; Journell, 2011; Subedi, 2006). Religious Christian teachers are positioned as (either knowingly or unwittingly) upholding the status quo of privileging the cultural norms of White Christianity in educational spaces. Two of these articles (Blumenfeld & Jaekel, 2012; Subedi, 2006) specifically discuss Christian privilege as a part of the hidden (and sometimes not-so-hidden) curriculum of U.S. schools.

Subedi's (2006) study of preservice teachers at a Midwestern university centers on "religious forms of discrimination" (p. 227) in schools—discrimination against certain forms of religion (generally non-Christian religions) that may also intersect with racial and ethnic prejudices. Subedi argues for increased conversations and education about religious diversity in teacher training. In Subedi's study, White female preservice teachers in early childhood education wrote reflections on how they encountered social difference in their field experiences, wrote cultural autobiographies, and participated in interviews. Subedi found that many of the Christian preservice teachers excused privileging of Christianity in public schools because the majority of the community shared the same values. Very little concern was given to the experience of minority groups in schools where Christianity was privileged.

The study linked preservice teachers' Christian religion with an unwillingness to be critical of how schools dealt with religion and religious issues (Christmas plays, Easter baskets, etc.). Additionally, Subedi found that preservice teachers who considered themselves to have a more politically engaged religion (i.e., they believed themselves to be working for equality as a part of their religious identity) often linked overseas missionary work that centered different religions as the "Other" with the concept of working for diversity and talking across differences in belief.

Another illustrative qualitative study would be Journell's (2011) study of six Chicago-area social studies teachers during the 2008 presidential election. Journell observed classrooms, interviewed teachers and students, and collected classroom artifacts to examine what election-related topics were considered "closed" for discussion and what topics were considered "open" for discussion. Open issues were considered to be issues that have more than one rational point of view, while closed issues had a generally accepted answer or point of view. Journell found that teachers made different decisions about what issues were considered open or closed and that the religious beliefs of the teachers affected their choices about how to treat certain issues. To clarify the researcher's definition of open or closed topics, an example would be discussions about Sarah Palin, the vice presidential candidate's gender. In all the classrooms observed, Palin's gender was "a closed issue in terms of her eligibility for the vice presidency, but the sexist comments made by students and teachers at each school suggest that . . . her gender was an open issue with respect to how they judged female politicians" (Journell, 2011, p. 348). Discussions of Palin did not center her gender as a disqualification for office, but her appearance was discussed as a pertinent factor in her candidacy in ways that male nominees' appearances were not.

Obama's religion was an issue that was treated less universally: "the only teachers who treated the fact that Obama's father had practiced Islam as an open issue were [two White male teachers], both of whom described themselves as devoutly religious" (Journell, 2011, p. 376). When students attempted to treat the matter as closed, one teacher adamantly shut down the conversation: "Would I want a Muslim in office? No way. Would I want a Buddhist in office? No way" (Journell, 2011, p. 377). In his discussion, Journell (2011) expresses concern that for teachers like the one quoted, who prided himself on teaching for diversity, religion may be so engrained in their belief systems that they may not realize the ways in which religion collides with their ability to inclusively teach civic engagement. In short, Journell states that this teacher's "theological certainty appeared to trump his other pedagogical decisions" (2011, p. 383). Journell's concern about the ability of devoutly Christian teachers to openly engage students in conversations about democratic principles (such as freedom of religion) without bias is illustrative of the aims of the articles in this category.

Whereas studies like Ahn et al.'s (2016; discussed earlier) viewed religious belief and discussion that centered religious values as a possible support for teachers who were attempting to enact social justice pedagogy, many articles positioned teachers' religious identity as a barrier to such practice. This is not to say that religious teachers and preservice teachers are positioned as wholly fixed in their identity as protectors of Christian privilege in these studies. Both of the articles that examine preservice teachers (Blumenfeld & Jaekel, 2012; Subedi, 2006) argue for an improved attention in preservice teacher education programs for more conversation, dialogue, and readings that invite preservice teachers to examine their own positionality and privilege not just regarding race, gender, and class but also religion. However, these articles uniformly approached religious teachers with some measure of suspicion. These researchers identified religious teachers as unwittingly problematic: Even when they were committed to social justice education in terms of equality of race and ethnicity, social class, or linguistic diversity, the teachers' religious beliefs were seen as consistently taking precedence over their students' diverse experiences as teachers made decisions about classroom practice.

Examining Teachers' Religious Identity Inside of Discourse

Not all studies of religious teachers position teachers' religious beliefs as an either/or proposition of wholly a problem or wholly an asset. Several studies worked to complicate current understandings of religious identity in teachers (Dedeoglu & Lamme, 2011; Huerta & Flemmer, 2005; Juzwik & McKenzie, 2015). These studies were often marked by a highly contextualized reading of religious teachers and students. Although researchers in these studies did not ignore the ways in which religious teachers' beliefs and practices may run counter to principles of multicultural or social justice education, these studies also acknowledged that many of the practices and beliefs of religious teachers are highly contextualized within communities of faith and are performed by teachers not with the intent of silencing others but with the intent of embodying their own beliefs and values. In short, these studies attend to the discourse that makes certain ways of being, knowing, and teaching possible.

These three studies (Dedeoglu & Lamme, 2011; Huerta & Flemmer, 2005; Juzwik & McKenzie, 2015) examined teacher identity in relation to teachers' ability to enact inclusive or multicultural pedagogies. The survey study of Dedeoglu and Lamme (2011) established that preservice teachers' religious beliefs (particularly when they are self-identified as conservative religious beliefs) do correlate with lower scores on a survey that was intended to measure students' attitudes toward diversity education (regarding race/ethnicity, gender, social class, sexual orientation, disabilities, language, and religion). Research like this may suggest that teachers who identify as conservatively religious may have a different understanding of the purpose of education—that is, that education may not be a project of diversity at all but, instead, a project of conversion to a single truth or a single way of being.

In Juzwik and McKenzie's (2015) portraiture study of two evangelical Christians (one a teacher, one a student) in a public school setting, the researchers construct portraits to invite a nuanced and measured stance toward both participants. These purposefully "complex portraits of religiously faithful persons in a particular classroom context" (Juzwik & McKenzie, 2015, p. 127) work to consider the limits of pluralistic education when students or teachers have "a deeply rooted resistance to open dialogue across ethical difference" (p. 145). Through a complicating examination of the writing of "This I Believe" essays in a public school classroom, Juzwik and McKenzie call for a reconceptualization of religious students and teachers—moving away from a deficit perspective towards religion and toward "strength-based strategy" (2015, p. 145). The researchers do not dismiss the importance of engaging students in ethical discourse with those who may not share their same ethical viewpoints, but they urge a complication of deficit narratives of religious teachers and students.

Huerta and Flemmer's (2005) study of preservice teachers who identify as members of the Church of Jesus Christ of Latter-day Saints (LDS; but more commonly known as Mormons) is another illustrative study that centers complication and context. In this multiple case study, the researchers examine how the religious beliefs and cultural practices of six White female LDS preservice teachers "inform and generate the identity and educational belief systems" (Huerta & Flemmer, 2005, p. 7) of these teachers, particularly as they prepared to teach in diverse communities. Each of the teachers in the study had expressed some interest or concern about living and teaching in more diverse communities than the one they had experienced growing up. As part of their secondary teacher preparation program, these preservice teachers read selections of multicultural literature, completed reflective writing assignments, practiced developing multicultural curriculum, and fulfilled two semesters of field experiences. Although the preservice teachers reported feeling more confident about their ability to design culturally relevant curricula and "were more willing to position themselves as active members of a diverse community" (Huerta & Flemmer, 2005, p. 12), they did not experience major paradigm shifts, nor did they feel obligated to question too deeply the political or social inequality that their belief system taught them to accept as the natural by-product of God-given agency.

An examination of one passage from this study further illuminates the characteristics of complicating approaches to teachers and their religious identities:

> Participants continued to support the notion that, if only non-members would follow the tenets of the LDS belief system, complex societal issues would need no further remedies. There would be no need for gender role and racial divisiveness, divorce, unemployment, homosexuality, and substance abuse. In their own LDS historical worldview, these participants believe immigrants can assimilate into American society and find success by their own merits in school. (Huerta & Flemmer, 2005, p. 12)

As in this excerpt, it was very common in complicating considerations of religious teachers for their beliefs to be represented not as outrageous or ridiculous but as a logical response to the doctrines of the belief system to which they belonged. In this study, the authors highly contextualized the religious beliefs of the participants by devoting a whole section (almost three pages) to an overview of the LDS Church's most important beliefs and practices (e.g., practices such as strict lifestyle guidelines like the Word of Wisdom and practicing daily prayer and scripture study and key beliefs like free agency or priesthood authority). Signal phrases such as "in their own LDS historical worldview" center religion as an identity category and as a contextual frame for the participants' beliefs. The study points out that "students' dedication to and reliance on their LDS roots is all encompassing" (Huerta & Flemmer, 2005, p. 3), including their identification of themselves as either having no culture or as identifying their religion as their culture. The contextualization of beliefs, generous reading of participants, and consideration of religion as an identity category in this study were representative of the studies in this category as a whole.

Professional Enactment of Religious Identity

What might be most relevant to the current study are studies that examine how religious teachers professionally enact their religious identities (Anderson et al., 2015; Hartwick, 2015a; Journell, 2011; Juzwik & McKenzie, 2015; White, 2014). These studies consider the connection between a teacher's practice in the classroom—what they actually do—and their religious beliefs. Journell's (2011) study of religious teachers' decisions on whether a topic was "open" or "closed" for classroom debate is an example of professional enactment because it explores *how* teachers' religious beliefs make their classroom practice possible—in this case, how they lead discussions or invite or dismiss student input. Anderson et al. (2015) found that preservice teachers' word choices while teaching about world religions showed an unwitting bias to Judeo-Christian religious traditions. Juzwik and McKenzie's (2015) portrait of an evangelical teacher explored the complex relationship between the teacher's unit planning, writing instruction, and student relationships and his Christian ethos of caring and community. Hartwick (2015a) drew a connection between teachers who identified as having a belief system with a strong "truth claim" as having less tendency to pose open-ended questions with multiple possible answers. In short, several studies have already worked to examine how teachers' beliefs didn't just affect their own identity as a teacher (a sense of calling or a responsibility to care for children) but also affected the *way* they taught (the words they chose, the lessons they planned, the questions they asked).

Additional studies connected teachers' personal religious beliefs with their identity as a teacher, particularly as a consideration of how teaching from a religious standpoint might influence many of the moral and ethical experiences that make teaching such a complicated profession. Several researchers (Huerta & Flemmer, 2005; White, 2010) highlight how teachers' religious beliefs influenced their moral ethical identity as a teacher. Huerta and Flemmer (2005; discussed earlier) concluded that links between preservice teachers' negative attitudes toward second-language learners and LGBTQ+ students correlated with specific doctrines of their religion, which had equally influenced legislation in the state in which they were teaching. White (2014) discussed links between teachers' beliefs about heaven and hell and their approach to classroom management—teachers who believed in heaven/hell were more likely to use reward systems whereas teachers who did not believe in heaven/hell were more likely to manage their classroom using a community problem-solving approach. Furthermore, White (2010) identifies areas of inquiry related to religion that teachers might use to guide their own exploration of their religious identity and its impact on their teaching, their ethical choices, and their student interactions.

Perhaps the most illustrative study is White's (2014) collective case study on the impact of teachers' religious beliefs on classroom management structures and practices. Using data collected from life-history interviews and classroom observations, White traced six elementary teachers' (Christian and Jewish) religious beliefs about mistakes and forgiveness, heaven and hell, and personal responsibility to others and then explicitly linked those beliefs to the setup of classroom management structures. For example, White drew parallels between teachers beliefs about heaven and hell and their approach to classroom management—teachers who believed in heaven/hell (evangelical Christians) were more likely to use reward systems whereas teachers who did not believe in heaven/hell (Quakers and Jews) were more likely to manage their classroom using a community problem-solving approach. White found that teachers' personal religious beliefs impacted their approach to community. Whereas Jewish teachers focused on peace, freedom, and justice as goals of community, Christian teachers referred to their call to love one another as a guiding principle for community building. Additionally, these religious teachers considered an apology and restitution to be an important part of students being able to learn from mistakes and receive forgiveness, a practice that White ties to Christian beliefs about repentance, atonement, and mercy and Jewish beliefs of reconciliation, reflection, and restoration. White's attention to not simply *what* teachers and preservice teachers believe but also *how* those beliefs make specific ethical and moral approaches to classroom situations commonsensical is an important contribution to complicating studies of religious teachers.

Discussion Relevant to the Current Study

The current study is, of course, influenced by previous research on the topic of religion and teachers. Quantitative research establishes the prevalence of religious teachers in the American public school system (Hartwick 2015a, 2015b; Slater, 2005) and the general underpreparedness of preservice teachers to discuss religions other than their own with much complexity or without bias (Anderson et al., 2015; Marks et al., 2014). The current study is an examination of secondary language arts classrooms—a place of study that has been underrepresented in existing scholarship on religious teachers (although Juzwik & McKenzie, 2015, and Skerrett, 2014, are welcome exceptions to the trend). However, there is some indication that religious literacy practices may influence broader literacy practices for religious youth (Rackley, 2014), including the purpose that is set for reading (reading for information or reading to make personal connections). Juzwik's (2014) description of the Bible-centered literacy practices of evangelicals suggests that the literacy practices they engage in in religious contexts center texts as authoritative (this affinity for authoritative texts might help explain why Hartwick, 2015b, found that religious teachers are more likely to use a textbook than are nonreligious teachers).

There are three most important takeaways from a review of pertinent literature for the current study. First, the pervasive influence of religion within American public schooling means that the very concept of teaching is imbued with Christian idealizations and discursive figurations. Second, Christian teachers feel like there are ethical mismatches between their identity as public school teachers and their identity as Christians. Third, teachers' religious identities and beliefs influence their teaching practice, including the texts they choose, the questions they ask (or don't ask), the discipline they enact, and the persona they project.

Notes

1. In 2009, the United States was the most religious nation in the industrialized world, with 89% of the population identifying as religious and 62% of the population identifying as highly religious. By comparison, 46% of the French population and 28% of the German and Austrian populations identified as religious (Brown, 2019).
2. This term was used in the original report of the study.
3. The researchers' conclusion that teacher education preparation has a duty to "prepare [teachers] for integrating their faith with their work" (Ahn et al., 2016, p. 49) bypasses several pertinent educational points of discussion without attending to their own assumptions, including what the purpose of public education is and what the role of teacher education is. While I might agree that teacher education should attend to preservice teachers' religious identities and the ethical issues they may encounter as part of their responsibilities as public school teachers, I question exactly what integration of faith with professional, publicly funded work might look like for teachers, and that is never spelled out by the researchers.

References

The AAR Religion in Schools Task Force. (2010). *Guidelines for teaching about religion in K–12 public schools in the United States.* American Academy of Religion. https://rlp.hds.harvard.edu/publications/guidelines-teaching-about-religion-k-12-public-schools-united-states

Abington School District v. Schempp, 374 U.S. 203 (1963).

Ahn, J., Hinson, D. W., & Teets, S. T. (2016). Teachers' views on integrating faith into their professional lives: A cross-cultural glimpse. *AILACTE Journal, 13*(1), 41–57.

Anderson, D., Mathys, H., & Cook, T. (2015). Religious beliefs, knowledge, and teaching actions: Elementary teacher candidates and world religions. *Religion & Education, 42*(3), 268–288.

Apple, M. W. (2013). *Teachers and texts: A political economy of class and gender relations in education.* Routledge.

Blumenfeld, W. J., & Jaekel, K. (2012). Exploring levels of Christian privilege awareness among preservice teachers. *Journal of Social Issues, 68*(1), 128–144.

Britton, E., Paine, L., Raizen, S., & Pimm, D. (2003). *Comprehensive teacher induction: Systems for early career learning.* Kluwer and WestEd.

Brown, M. H. (2009, December 16). U.S. is most religious in industrialized world. *Baltimore Sun.* https://www.baltimoresun.com/bs-mtblog-2009-12-united_states_is_most_religiou-story.html

Bruce, R. T., & Bailey, B. (2014). Religious issues in English education: An examination of the field. *Religion & Education, 41*(3), 310–328.

Burke, K. J., & Segall, A. (2015). Teaching as Jesus making: The hidden curriculum of Christ in schooling. *Teachers College Record, 117*(3), 1–27.

Burke, K. J., & Segall, A. (2017). *Christian privilege in U. S. education: Legacies and current issues.* Routledge.

Butler, J. (2004). Imitation and gender insubordination. In The Judith Butler Reader, edited by Sara Salih and Judith Butler. (Malden, MA: Blackwell Publishing, 2004): 119-137.

Butler, J. (2015). Imitation and gender insubordination. In A. Garry & M. Pearsall (Eds.), *Women, knowledge and reality: Explorations in feminist philosophy* (pp. 371–387). Routledge.

Calvert, K. (2013, January 9). Promoting Hinduism? Parents demand removal of school yoga class. In *Morning Edition*. NPR. https://www.npr.org/2013/01/09/168613461/promoting-hinduism-parents-demand-removal-of-school-yoga-class

Campbell, P., & Crowe, C. (2015). *Spirituality in young adult literature: The last taboo*. Rowman & Littlefield.

Carper, J. C., & Hunt, T. C. (2011). Taking religion seriously: Another approach. *Religion & Education, 38*(1), 81–89.

Dedeoglu, H., & Lamme, L. L. (2011). Selected demographics, attitudes, and beliefs about diversity of preservice teachers. *Education and Urban Society, 43*(4), 468–485.

DelFattore, J. (2004). *The fourth R: Conflicts over religion in America's public schools*. Yale University Press.

Derrida, J. (1997). *Deconstruction in a nutshell: A conversation with Jacques Derrida* (J. D. Caputo, Ed.). Fordham University Press.

Derrida, J. (2001). Talking liberties: Jacques Derrida's interview with Alan Montefiore. In G. J. Biesta & D. Egea-Kuehne (Eds.), *Derrida & education* (pp. 176–185). Routledge.

Durkheim, E. (1965). *The elementary forms of the religious life* (J. Swain, Trans.). Free Press. (Original work published 1915)

Grissmer, D. W., & Kirby, S. N. (1987). *Teacher attrition: The uphill climb to staff the nation's schools*. RAND.

Guillemette, L., & Cossette, J. (2006). *Deconstruction and différance*. Sign. http://www.signosemio.com/derrida/deconstruction-and-differance.asp

Hadley, H. L., & Fassbender, W. J. (2020). Recognizing religious identity in preservice teachers. In M. Juzwik, D. Davila, J. Stone, & K. Burke (Eds.), *Christian religious literacies: Histories, implications and alternative readings* (pp. 37–50). Routledge.

Hartwick, J. M. (2015a). Public school teachers' beliefs in and conceptions of God: What teachers believe and why it matters. *Religion & Education, 42*(2), 122–146.

Hartwick, J. M. (2015b). Teacher prayerfulness: Identifying public school teachers who connect their spiritual and religious lives with their professional lives. *Religion & Education, 42*(1), 54–80.

Haynes, C. C. (2012). Getting religion right in public schools. *Kappan, 93*(4), 8–14.

Hobson, A. J., Ashby, P., Malderez, A., & Tomlinson, P. D. (2009). Mentoring beginning teachers: What we know and what we don't. *Teaching and Teacher Education, 25*(1), 207–216.

Huerta, G., & Flemmer, L. (2005). Identity, beliefs and community: LDS (Mormon) pre-service secondary teacher views about diversity. *Intercultural Education, 16*(1), 1–14.

Ingersoll, R. (2003). *Is there really a teacher shortage?* Consortium for Policy Research in Education, University of Pennsylvania. http://www.gse.upenn.edu/pdf/rmi/Shortage-RMI-09-2003.pdf

Ingersoll, R., & May, H. (2011). *Recruitment, retention and the minority teacher shortage*. Consortium for Policy Research in Education, University of Pennsylvania.

Ingersoll, R., & Strong, M. (2011). The impact of induction and mentoring programs for beginning teachers: A critical review of the research. *Review of Educational Research, 81*(2), 201–233.

James, J. H. (2015). Toward democratic living and learning. In J. H. James (Ed.), *Religion in the classroom: Dilemmas for democratic education* (pp. XX–XX). Routledge.

Journell, W. (2011). Teachers' controversial issue decisions related to race, gender, and religion during the 2008 presidential election. *Theory and Research in Social Education, 39*(3), 348–392.

Juzwik, M. M. (2014). American evangelical biblicism as literate practice: A critical review. *Reading Research Quarterly, 49*(3), 335–349.

Juzwik, M. M., & McKenzie, C. (2015). Writing, religious faith, and rooted cosmopolitan dialogue: Portraits of two American evangelical men in a public school English classroom. *Written Communication, 32*(2), 121–149.

Kunzman, R. (2006). *Grappling with the good: Talking about religion and morality in public schools.* State University of New York Press.

Ladson-Billings, G. (1994). *The dreamkeepers: Successful teachers of African American students.* Jossey-Bass.

Ladson-Billings, G. (2000). Fighting for our lives: Preparing teachers to teach African American students. *Journal of Teacher Education, 51*(3), 206–214.

Landau, J. (2014, January 7). California first-grader barred from distributing candy canes with religious message. *New York Daily Times.* http://www.nydailynews.com/news/national/teacher-throws-first-grader-gift-honoring-jesus-article-1.1568951

Lemon v. Kurtzman, 403 U. S. 602 (1971).

Marks, M. J., Binkley, R., & Daly, J. K. (2014). Preservice teachers and religion: Serious gaps in religious knowledge and the first amendment. *The Social Studies, 105*(5), 245–256.

Nash, R. J. (2001). *Religious pluralism in the academy: Opening the dialogue.* Peter Lang.

National Center for Education Statistics. (2017). *Characteristics of public primary and secondary school teachers in the United States: Results from the 2015–16 national teacher and principal survey.* https://nces.ed.gov/programs/coe/pdf/coe_clr.pdf

Newman, L. L. (2004). Faith, spirituality, and religion: A model for understanding the differences. *The College of Student Affairs Journal,* 23(2), 102–110.

Nieto, S. (1996). *Affirming diversity: The sociopolitical context for multicultural education.* Longman.

Nord, W. A. (2010). *Does God make a difference? Taking God seriously in our schools and universities.* Oxford University Press.

Nord, W. A., & Haynes, C. C. (1998). *Taking religion seriously across the curriculum.* Association for Supervision and Curriculum Development.

Picower, B. (2009). The unexamined Whiteness of teaching: How White teachers maintain and enact dominant racial ideologies. *Race Ethnicity and Education, 12*(2), 197–215.

Rackley, E. D. (2014). Scripture based discourses of Latter-day Saint and Methodist youths. *Reading Research Quarterly,* 49(4), 417–435.

Rogers, M. (2011). Teaching about religion in public schools: Where do we go from here? *Religion & Education, 38*(1), 38–47.

Skerrett, A. (2014). Religious literacies in a secular literacy classroom. *Reading Research Quarterly,* 49(2), 233–250.

Slater, R. O. (2008). American teachers: What do they believe? *Education Next, 8*(1), 46–52.

Smith, J. Z. (1995). Religion, definition of. In J. Z. Smith (Ed.), *The HarperCollins dictionary of religion* (pp. 893–894). HarperCollins.

Stempel, J. (2017, August 23). *Washington football coach cannot pray after games: U.S. appeals court.* Reuters. https://www.reuters.com/article/us-washington-coach/washington-football-coach-cannot-pray-after-games-u-s-appeals-court-idUSKCN1B32B1

Subedi, B. (2006). Preservice teachers' beliefs and practices: Religion and religious diversity. *Equity & Excellence in Education, 39*(3), 227–238.

Waggoner, M. D. (2016). Educating about religion toward a "more perfect Union." *Religion and Education,* 43(2), 125–126.

Weaver, H. L. (2017, December 18). *Proselytizing public school official: "I'll stop when someone makes me stop."* ACLU. https://www.aclu.org/blog/religious-liberty/religion-and-public-schools/proselytizing-public-school-official-ill-stop

White, K. R. (2009). Connecting religion and teacher identity: The unexplored relationship between religion and teachers in public schools. *Teaching and Teacher Education, 25*(6), 857–866.

White, K. R. (2010). Asking sacred questions: Understanding religion's impact on teacher belief and action. *Religion & Education, 37*(1), 40–59.

White, K. R. (2014). Community, forgiveness, and the golden rule: The impact of teachers' religious identities on classroom management structures. *Religion & Education, 41*(1), 63–79.

CHAPTER TWO

In the Spirit of Inquiry: Ethics and Hospitality

MUCH OF THIS BOOK centers on the notion of moments of hesitation of evangelical Christian teachers (particularly in English language arts classrooms). These moments of hesitation are not unique to only evangelical Christian teachers—most teachers acknowledge that interactions with students are complex and require careful ethical consideration. Edgoose (2001) offers an example of a moment of hesitation that nearly all teachers will recognize: A teacher has been working to motivate and reach a resistant student and is finally seeing progress and engagement. The dilemma comes at the end-of-term grade: Should the teacher strike a deal to grade the student based only on the work completed and ignore all the missing work from the first part of the semester? If the teacher grades all the work from the semester, the student will fail. If the teacher grades only the completed portion, is that fair to students who completed all the assignments for the whole semester? Educational ethics texts might help the teacher weigh whether they should bend assessment norms for an individual student "in terms of consequences (probably 'yes'), duty ('no'), and caring ('yes')" (Edgoose, 2001, p. 120). But the teacher already knows what the choices are: either bend the rules or don't. Using an approach that centers the ethics of care or the ethics of duty or the ethics of consequence offers little "to the educator caught [between the opposing choices] save a justification" (Edgoose, 2001, p. 125). A moment of hesitation is the term that I give to that feeling of being caught, of weighing choices against responsibility and care and consequence.

Moments of hesitation describe the space before a decision has to be made—particularly a decision that feels impossible to navigate ethically. I do not mean moments when the right choice is imminently clear but hard to make because of possible consequences. Instead, I'm talking about moments where there is a feeling of uncertainty about what *should* be done, a hesitation over how to navigate an ethically tricky moment. Edgoose (2001) states that when teachers are "in a hesitant moment—as when one is in the moment of a just decision—one is ethically exposed" because "one is unsure of one's own boundaries and the limits of one's liability" (p. 130). These moments when teachers are hesitatingly moving toward just decisions by weighing the various demands and limits placed on them are important moments to examine because they are moments of ethical vulnerability and exposure. They are moments when teachers must most fully reckon with the responsibilities and commitments of their own ways of being and interacting with the students (and, more broadly, the world) around them. Edgoose asserts that these moments of hesitation "riddle our educational experiences, and yet they are all-too-often invisible to our critical studies of the classroom" (2001, p. 131).

To make these moments of hesitation more visible, this study draws heavily (and most broadly) from poststructural conceptions of discourse. More specifically, I turn to Derrida's writings on ethics and hospitality to more fully plumb moments of hesitation and the interplay between teachers' responsibilities to themselves, to their students, to their employers, and to their God. Derrida's consideration of ethics is particularly valuable because it provides a "language of ethics that takes the impasse of the dilemma seriously and offers the educator better understanding of the dilemma itself" (Edgoose, 2001, p. 125). The focus on evangelical teachers' moments of hesitation is a nod to the seriousness of the dilemmas they weigh in their classroom practice; it is an acknowledgment that the impasses they feel matter within the larger educational discourse. But these teachers' moments of hesitation are also offered up to invite educators to more fully examine the dilemma itself: to reckon with what it means to be a part of the "vulnerable responsibility of education" (Edgoose, 2001, p. 123).

Discourse

I use poststructural conceptions of discourse to make space for a generous yet critical reading of my participants and their performance as teachers in public school systems. Although the term *discourse* has long described the act of speaking and communicating, poststructuralist theorists and scholars (Bové, 1990; Butler, 2013; Foucault, 1971/1966; among many others) use the term *discourse* to describe "a particular way of talking about and understanding the world (or an aspect of the world)" (Philips & Jorgensen, 2002, p. 1). What makes the poststructuralist approach to discourse unique is an understanding of discourse as both limiting and constitutive. Discourse, or the way we talk about the world, makes certain ways of thinking and being possible while making other ways of thinking and being impossible. Discourse is not neutral then—it marks the limits and makes possible new figurations of being, speaking, and performing.

For poststructuralists, discourses are always tied up in power because discourse creates systems, disciplines, and institutions that are supported by the discourse and, in turn, support the discourse. Discourse and power do not necessarily have only negative connotations here (also a feature of poststructural understandings of discourse) because power can be used to support discourses, to challenge discourses, and to change discourses. This is particularly relevant to this study concerning the religious discourse of evangelical Christianity, which is both ideological and material: Christian discourse makes certain ways of thinking possible and, more important, self-evident or sensical, but it also gives rise to a whole industry which works to maintain or challenge the regulatory discourse of Christianity: churches, pastors, parsonages, religious self-help books, youth groups, national conventions, seminaries, and religiopolitical think tanks, to name a few. Poststructuralists' understanding of human meaning-making as a product of discourse and discursive figurations means that truth claims, and especially universal truth claims, are highly suspect. Bové (1990) explains that "all 'truths' are relative to the frame of reference which contains them; more radically, 'truths' are a function of these frames; and even more radically, these discourses 'constitute' the truths they claim to discover and transmit" (p. 56). What makes discourse so powerful, then, is how discourse creates truths that within the discourse are, as Bové, calls it *commonsensical* or *self-evident*. Foucault (1966/1971) refers to the same discursive constructions that make certain ways of thinking and being possible as the *grid of intelligibility*; Laclau (1995), drawing on Kant, might call it the *conditions of possibility*. Derrida (2001b) points out, too, that discourse is not ever completely closed to reinterpretations and reconfigurations; discourse has the possibility of "a field of infinite substitutions" (p. 289).

A poststructural approach to discourse makes several underlying approaches to this particular study possible. First, framing participants as both products and participants in discursive figurations and practices makes possible a simultaneously critical and generous approach to the participants' performance of evangelical Christian teachers in public education classrooms. Instead of framing some of the participants' beliefs and practices as shocking or outrageous (although they may seem so to me, within my own discursive framework as a fairly liberal education instructor), a discursive analysis situates these beliefs and practices as sensical within the discourse that created them. This does not mean that certain beliefs and practices are not problematic but simply offers a way of viewing beliefs and practices as a product of discourse. I do not, of course, wish to minimize the possibility of resistance and reconfiguration of discourse by the participants. Nor do I believe that taking an underlying theoretical understanding of discourse means that I cannot acknowledge that certain participant beliefs and practices are problematic within the larger educational discourse. For Derrida, discourses are meant to be examined, critiqued, challenged, problematized, loosened, and, of course, *deconstructed* with the possibility of new constructions and new performances.

Derridean Deconstruction

I first turned to Derrida to consider some of the tensions that surfaced from the initial study that William Fassbender and I (Hadley & Fassbender, 2020) conducted with evangelical preservice teachers. As part of that study, we found that participants felt their religious identities were silenced in their teacher education classrooms. I was equally troubled by the participants' stance toward LGBTQ+ students in their own classrooms. As an example, one participant reported, "I can't have a[n LGBTQ+] student coming to me telling me that they need my support . . . and actually give them support" (Hadley & Fassbender, 2020, p. 47). That statement, and others like it, felt like a silencing of a different identity. These findings caused me to consider what it means to responsibly construct[1] another human being in the context of teacher education. Teacher education is a project that makes a very concerted effort to construct, through our (teacher educators') interactions with teacher candidates, a certain type of teacher with a certain set of beliefs and classroom practices. It's a part of the profession, and if I was going to contribute to the regulatory discourse of what makes a *good* teacher (and I don't think I, or other teacher educators, can or should remove ourselves from this discourse), I wanted to think about how I might construct fellow teacher educators and future teachers in a responsible and generous way in my interactions with them. As a teacher educator, I felt very torn about how I might construct the future teachers I worked with—there seemed to me to be a split responsibility to the future teachers themselves and to the many individuals who would be a part of their future classrooms. How could I model for my evangelical students what it means to accept *all* students into their classroom if I wasn't willing to accept their religious identity in my classroom? But if I did unconditionally accept their religious identity and welcome their religious ways of knowing and being—which includes, of course, religiously informed transphobia and homophobia—into my teacher education classroom, would they turn around and create classrooms that excluded LGBTQ+ students? What was my responsibility to the students/future teachers in front of me? What was my responsibility to the students who would one day be in their classrooms? This dichotomy between responsibility to the individual and responsibility to the universal is an important element in my interest in evangelical Christian teachers and informs a great deal of my work as a teacher educator. In Derrida's deconstruction of the concepts of hospitality and ethics, I find space to fully plumb (although perhaps to never fully resolve) the inherent tensions in my own positionality as a researcher, my conception of my research participants, and my methodological choices.

The Other, Deconstruction, and Hospitality

Derrida's conception of the other is based in a deconstruction of the subject, which is a historical tracing of how the human being came to be understood as "the subject of his or her own experience, life, activity, responsibilities and so on" (Montefiore, 2001, p. 177). For Derrida (2001a), the concept of otherness springs from historical configurations of subjectivity—deconstruction invites an affirmation of difference while still saying, "*Yes*, I *speak* to you, I *address* you, I *listen* to you" (p. 180). Deconstruction of the subject allows for a welcoming of the other, for the creation of an "attentiveness to otherness, to the alterity of the other, to something new and other" (p. 180). This is why deconstruction is sometimes defined most simply as a respect for the other (Anderson, 2012; Caputo, 1997; Sinha, 2013).

Welcoming of the other ties directly to Derrida's deconstruction of the concept of hospitality (Derrida 1997/2001), a term that he prefers over the term *tolerance* when exploring the historical configurations of what it means to welcome the other. For Derrida, who draws heavily on Kant's work here, ethics *is* hospitality, and hospitality "is culture itself and not simply one ethic amongst others" (Derrida 1997/2001, p. 16). As one expects from Derrida, he sees a tautology, an aporia, an impossibility in the enactment of absolute hospitality—an aporia contained within the word itself. Derrida has described an aporia as the space between the possible and impossible; often when Derrida uses the term *aporia*, he presents a sort of possible–impossible paradox. For example, he examines the concept of true selfless *giving* as a concept whose possibility is only possible in its impossibility. In the case of hospitality, Derrida points out that the word derives from the Latin word for stranger (*hospes*) and evolved in other words to mean enemy (*hostile*) when combined with the Latin *pets*, which means to have power (*pot*ential, *pot*ent; Caputo, 1997). Built into the word *hospitality* is the impossibility Derrida seeks to capture: How does one wholeheartedly welcome a guest or stranger (*hospes*) while remaining in power (*pets*) as the head of the household?

Derrida's careful examination of the responsibilities and commitments of hospitality, both in philosophical and religious literature—a deconstruction of what hospitality has come to mean and what sociopolitical commitments are hidden within the concept itself—opens up space for possibility within an impossibility. What Derridean deconstruction of hospitality makes space for are new performances of hospitality that trouble the limits of an unlimited welcome and question whether the foundational understandings of what it means to be hospitable might be reworked and reconfigured.

Derrida traces the concept of hospitality by examining the writings of Sophocles, the stories of Oedipus and Antigone, and the biblical story of Lot and his daughters. At its most simple, what Derrida finds in these foundational pieces is that hospitality is a welcoming in of the other, of the foreigner. Absolute hospitality, Derrida (1997/2000) points out,

> requires that I open my home and I give not only to the foreigner . . . but to the absolute, unknown, anonymous other, and that I *give place* to them, that I let them come, that I let them arrive, and take place in the place I offer them, without asking of them either reciprocity or even their names. (p. 25)

Hospitality, under Derrida's methodical deconstruction, could never be just that simple, of course. Derrida sees in hospitality multiple aporetic constructions. The unlimited, absolute nature of hospitality always must be limited. There can be no hospitality without *finitude*, or without some limit to demarcate the beginning and the end of hospitality. If there is no finitude, the receiver of hospitality is no longer a welcomed other, but a parasite (we can think, here, of Penelope's suitors in *The Odyssey* [Homer, 1919], who trespassed the hospitality of Odysseus's home for years on end). There can equally be no hospitality without *sovereignty*, or without the power of the host to make decisions about when and to whom hospitality is offered. The host must be in possession of his[2] own house to offer hospitality because what will the host offer if he has nothing to offer at all.

Thus, finitude and sovereignty are not only essential characteristics of hospitality, but they are also the characteristics that make it possible for violence to be enacted within hospitality. Derrida (1997/2000) points out that

> since there is no hospitality without finitude, sovereignty can only be exercised by filtering, choosing, and thus by excluding and doing violence. Injustice, a certain injustice . . . begins right away, from the very threshold of the right to hospitality. (p. 55)

Hospitality—to be hospitality, to be a freely given gift from host to hosted—implies an inequality, a power imbalance, an ability to give to someone who has nothing *in this place*. What we might consider for the religious teachers in this study is how they define hospitality: To whom do they offer hospitality; how do they filter, choose, and exclude others from hospitality; and what criteria do they use to determine who is an other who is eligible to receive hospitality and who is an other who is not eligible?

An essential piece of Derrida's (1997/2000) deconstruction of hospitality is his consideration of the moment of arrival, or the moment when a *stranger*, a *foreigner*, an *other* appears on the horizon and makes hospitality necessary. Importantly, or of particular interest to this study, the stranger/foreigner/other may speak a different language, may require a certain amount of forbearance or tolerance with their otherness, may test the limits of hospitality by virtue of their very otherness. The stranger may be one who questions. The stranger may ask different questions than have been asked before. The stranger may even be one whose questions disturb the comfortable way of thinking and doing and being that have been established in this place, by these people who must now offer hospitality. Derrida says that the stranger/foreigner/other "shakes up the threatening dogmatism of the paternal *logos*: the being that is, and the being that is not" (1997/2000, p. 5). The appearance of a stranger or an other requires a recalibration of who is a being, who is eligible to receive hospitality, and who is instead—as Derrida terms it—a barbarian or a *wholly* other or a being that is not. These recalibrations are, of course, based on considerations of who is counted to be the subject of their own experiences and are highly contextualized within sociopolitical frameworks. These moments of decision can lead to moments of violence, refusals to forbear, or failures of hospitality.

For evangelical Christian teachers, this moment of arrival is equally important. How and why are they determining who is a stranger and who is a "being that is not" (Derrida, 1997/2000, p. 5)? What sociopolitical frameworks shape their understandings of the stranger and the "being that is not?" How might the act of teaching in pluralistic public school settings challenge them to recalibrate their considerations of who is a being and who is a "being that is not?" How might they identify themselves as strangers, foreigners, or others in public school settings?

Language, too, plays a role in the Derridean (1978; 1997/2000) conception of hospitality, and the question of to whom hospitality is offered. The stranger/foreigner/other asks for hospitality in a language that is not his own—"the one imposed on him by the master of the house, the host, the king, the lord, the authorities, the nation, the State, the father, etc." (Derrida, 1997/2000, p. 15). Translation, then—and here we might consider translation to include not only customs and behavioral norms, of course, but also expectations of the sacred and the profane (Durkheim, 1915/1965), religious beliefs and practices—becomes the first act of violence within the concept of hospitality. Derrida insists this is also where the first question about the limits of hospitality begins: "Must we ask the foreigner to understand us, to speak our language, in all the sense of this term, in all its possible extensions, before being able . . . to welcome him into our country?" (Derrida, 1997/2000, p. 15). Moreover, language is what makes possible the determination of a being from a "being that is not," as the foreigner is asked to make plain his proper name and his place of birth to make clear the way in which he is to be addressed before he is offered hospitality.

And here is where Derrida (1997/2000) sees another limit to hospitality, another boundary on the supposedly unbounded welcome. Drawing on Levinas, Derrida says that language *is* hospitality:

> Nevertheless, we have come to wonder whether absolute, hyperbolic, unconditional hospitality doesn't consist in suspending language, a particular determinate language, and even the address to the other. Shouldn't we also submit to a sort of holding back of the temptation to ask the other who he is, what her name is, where he comes from, etc.? Shouldn't we abstain from asking another these questions, which herald so many required conditions, and thus limits, to a hospitality thereby constrained and thereby confined into a law and a duty? (Derrida, 1997/2000, p. 135)

What Derrida is questioning, here, and throughout his deconstruction of hospitality, might best be phrased as an exploration of whether hospitality might look different if we choose to perform it differently. "Are we the heirs to this tradition of hospitality? Up to what point?" asks Derrida (1997/2000, p. 155) as a conclusion as well as a beginning. The end of Derridean deconstruction, the moment when the aporia or the impossibility has been plumbed deeply, is always already an opening or an entry point to possibility. What if, for example, we choose to perform a new version of hospitality? What might this new performance make possible? What might be impossible? Derrida views the deconstruction of the concept of hospitality as an opening up, a challenge to create something new, to push the bounds of what hospitality does mean and what it might mean. Recognizing the inherent (im)possibility of fulfilling wholly our responsibility to the other isn't intended to be a hopeless or fruitless task but, instead, is meant to propel us to *do* something, to performatively challenge the impossibility of hospitality.

In this exploration of evangelical teachers, I use Derridean conceptions of hospitality to consider how teachers' religious beliefs make certain performances of hospitality (im)possible. How do the discursive figurations and practices of their religious identities allow them to include, filter, exclude, and make sense of who is a being and who is a "being that is not." Considerations of finitude and sovereignty, the language and violence of hospitality, the conditions that make an arrival of the other possible allow for a complex (and often troubled) understanding of the way evangelical teachers are constructing themselves and their students in public classroom spaces.

For this study, which examines the tensions that new teachers may feel between the two different (and sometimes contradictory) discursive formations of religious calling and public educator, Derrida's conception of hospitality seems of particular pertinence. How can teachers performatively challenge the impossibility of hospitality without first recognizing and challenging their own alterity? The too-easy parallel of a teacher as the host of the classroom, welcoming in the other embodied in each student, should also be more carefully examined. Derrida certainly did not intend the role of host to only apply to people in positions of authority or the role of other to only apply to those with less power. Instead, teachers are all always host *and* other. The deconstruction of the concept of hospitality is not just a metaphor for how classrooms might work—it can instead be thought of as an examination of ethical behavior as a teacher and as a learner.

Aporetic Ethics and Evangelical Christian Teachers

As I designed this study, it was important to me to engage the participants with some of the ideas and theory that informed my own thinking around the topic. Because I was interested in understanding the participants' decisions through a Derridean lens, I turned to Derrida's deconstruction of ethics, justice, and lawfulness to guide my conversations with participants about their moments of hesitation where they felt pulled by sometimes-competing demands between their teaching identities and their identities as evangelical Christians. It is worth noting that participants were introduced to this Derridean framework of ethics and decision-making during our first focus group (more on that later) to guide our conversations about how a moment of hesitation might be defined. We also used this framework in interviews to talk through how participants accounted (or didn't account) for the aporias that Derrida identifies in the concept of ethical decisions. I give an overview here of the framework that guided participants' understanding of a moment of hesitation and their own choices within those moments.

Because Derrida has, at times, equated ethics with hospitality (Caputo, 1997; Derrida, 1997/2001) and equated deconstruction with justice (Derrida, 1992; Miedema & Biesta, 2004) and has equally declared both hospitality and justice to be aporetic concepts (if not impossibilities), one can almost excuse Derridean critics for representing deconstruction as a Nietzschean-anything-goes free-for-all. However, to do so is to misunderstand Derrida's belief that possibility is born from impossibility, that the impossibility of justice, hospitality, and responsibility is what opens these conceptions up to new configurations, to new challenges to their intelligibility, and, ultimately, to new performances of these conceptions.

In *Force of Law*, Derrida (1992) lays out three aporias that must be accounted for in any decision: the *aporia of (in)decision*, the *aporia of singularity*, and the *aporia of urgency*. In the case of ethical decision, all three aporias (decision, singularity, and urgency) rely on the conception of *justice* as fundamentally different from the concept of *lawful* and different again from the concept of *right*. Derrida draws distinctions between what is legal and what is just; if they were the same, he argues, we would require not *judges*, who are instructed to consider context, circumstance, and singularity, but *calculators*, because legality is a simple matter of determining what law was broken and assigning the prescripted penalty laid forth in the law.

The *aporia of (in)decision*, then, describes the condition of a "decision [that] turns on undecidability" (Anderson, 2012, p. 80). For a decision to actually, in fact, be a decision, it must be more than an application of a rule or a guideline. For Derrida then, every case is other, every case requires a new calibration between existing rules and unique interpretations, and a responsible or just decision requires attention to the uneven and singular nature of decisions themselves. Within just decisions, Derrida insists that *the aporia of singularity* must be accounted for: how to balance universal responsibility with "the singularity of the other" (Derrida, 1992, p. 20). Although Derrida conceptualizes "responsibility without limits" (1992, p. 19), he also acknowledges that we are constantly making choices about *who* or *what* we sacrifice in order to be responsible to the singular individual.

The third aporia present in every decision is the *aporia of urgency*. Quite simply, this aporia insists that although it is impossible to make an entirely just or an entirely ethical decision (because of the impossibility of decision and the impossibility of attending simultaneously to singularity and multiplicity), *a decision must be made*. To continuously defer decisions, to allow the impossibility of justice to paralyze decision-making indefinitely, is another form of irresponsibility, so decisions must be urgent. The necessity of action doesn't necessarily forestall the importance of the aporias of decision and singularity, but it does require a reckoning, a *true* decision whereby one is both aware of *who* is othered in that decision and *what* is being privileged.

Derridean deconstruction is a workable theoretical framework for evangelical Christian classroom teachers and educational researchers, particularly around complex issues. For this study, I primarily used Derrida's deconstruction of hospitality to understand and frame my thinking and analysis of the choices of the participants. However, I asked the participants to frame their moments of hesitation using Derrida's deconstruction of ethics and decisions—to think about all three of the aporias Derrida identifies in ethical decision-making. As part of our first focus group, the participants and I talked through Derrida's deconstruction of ethics, and then participants shared instances that had happened in their classroom where they hesitated because of one of these aporias: decidability, responsibility to the multiple and the singular, and urgency (see Figure 2.1 for the handout I used to walk participants through these concepts). I chose to talk through Derridean aporias of decision-making with the participants to create a shared language to describe and examine the kind of complicated ethical calculations I am most interested in researching.

A Derridean approach to my research—focusing not on what the *right* answer is, but on what the possibilities are, centering moments of hesitation (mine but perhaps, more important, new teachers')—provided both a shared language and the conceptual focus to guide my research. Using Derrida's conceptions of deconstruction, focusing on teachers' moments of hesitation allowed me to frame my research "not [as] an unmasking but [as] a keeping open, alive, loose, on guard against itself" (Lather, 2004, p. 6). To be clear, then, participants used Derrida's deconstruction of ethics to guide *their* thinking in this study about what a moment of hesitation was, what context influenced their decisions. However, I used a Derridean deconstruction of hospitality to make sense of the commitments of the decisions that the participants reported as moments of hesitation in their own teaching, particularly in how those decisions related to welcoming in the other and making decisions about who is a welcome guest and who is a "being that

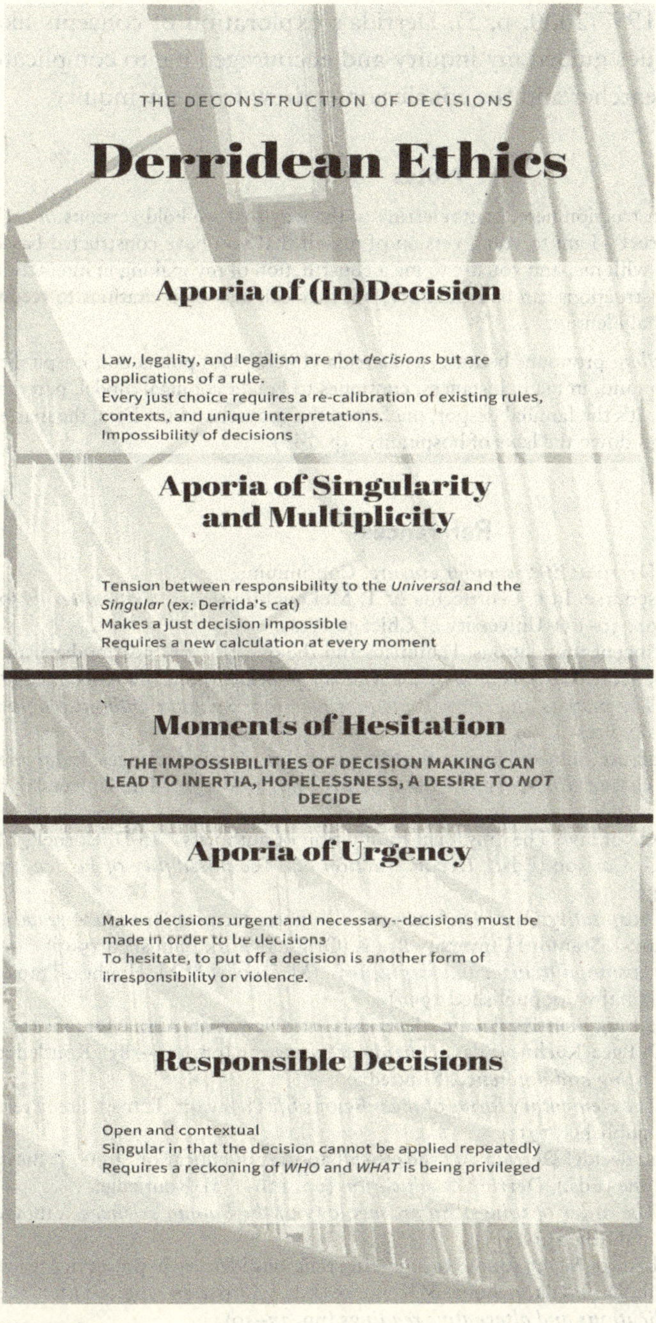

THE DECONSTRUCTION OF DECISIONS

Derridean Ethics

Aporia of (In)Decision

Law, legality, and legalism are not *decisions* but are applications of a rule.
Every just choice requires a re-calibration of existing rules, contexts, and unique interpretations.
Impossibility of decisions

Aporia of Singularity and Multiplicity

Tension between responsibility to the *Universal* and the *Singular* (ex: Derrida's cat)
Makes a just decision impossible
Requires a new calculation at every moment

Moments of Hesitation

THE IMPOSSIBILITIES OF DECISION MAKING CAN LEAD TO INERTIA, HOPELESSNESS, A DESIRE TO *NOT* DECIDE

Aporia of Urgency

Makes decisions urgent and necessary--decisions must be made in order to be decisions
To hesitate, to put off a decision is another form of irresponsibility or violence.

Responsible Decisions

Open and contextual
Singular in that the decision cannot be applied repeatedly
Requires a reckoning of *WHO* and *WHAT* is being privileged

Figure 2.1.

is not" (Derrida, 1997/2000, p. 5). Derrida's exploration of concepts like hospitality and ethics guided my inquiry and encouraged me to complicate my stance as a researcher and the conclusions I drew from my inquiry.

Notes

1. When I speak of construction here, I am referring to the way that we hold versions of each other that we construct—I am to you a version of myself that you have constructed based on your experiences with me, and you are to me a construction of my making in interaction with you. These constructions can be regulatory, but they can also be invitations to reconfigurations of personal identity.
2. I use here the *he/his/him* pronouns because, as Derrida (1997/2000) points out, hospitality has historically been (and, in many instances, continues to be) "a conjugal model, paternal and phallogocentric. It's the familial despot, the father, the spouse, and the boss, the master of the house who lays down the laws of hospitality" (p. 149).

References

Anderson, N. (2012). *Derrida: Ethics under erasure.* Continuum.

Bové, P. A. (1990). Discourse. In F. Lentricchia & T. McLaughlin (Eds.), *Critical terms for literary study* (pp. 50–65). University of Chicago Press.

Butler, J. (2013). Contingent foundations: Feminism and the question of "postmodernism." In J. Butler & J. Scott (Eds.), *Feminists theorize the political* (pp. 21–39). Routledge.

Caputo, J. D. (1997). *The prayers and tears of Jacques Derrida: Religion without religion.* Indiana University Press.

Derrida, J. (1978). Structure, sign and play in the discourse of the human sciences. In *Jacques Derrida, Writing and difference* (A. Bass, Trans.; pp. 278–293). The University of Chicago Press.

Derrida, J. (1992). Force of law: The "mystical foundation of authority." In D. Cornell, M. Rosenfeld, & G. Carlson (Eds.), *Deconstruction and the possibility of justice* (pp. 3–67). Routledge.

Derrida, J. (2000). *Of hospitality: Anne Dufourmantelle invites Jacques Derrida to respond* (R. Bowlby, Trans.). Stanford University Press. (Original work published 1997)

Derrida, J. (2001). *On cosmopolitanism and forgiveness.* (M. Dooley & M. Hughes, Trans.). Routledge. (Original work published 1997)

Derrida, J. (2001a). Talking liberties: Jacques Derrida's interview with Alan Montefiore. In G. J. Biesta & D. Egea-Kuehne (Eds.), *Derrida & education* (pp. 176–185). Routledge.

Derrida, J. (2001b). *Writing and difference.* Routledge.

Durkheim, E. (1965). *The elementary forms of the religious life* (J. Swain, Trans.). Free Press. (Original work published 1915)

Edgoose, J. (2001). Just decide! Derrida and the ethical aporias of education. In G. J. Biesta & D. Egea-Kuehne (Eds.), *Derrida & education* (pp. 119–133). Routledge.

Foucault, M. (1971). *The order of things: An archaeology of the human sciences.* Vintage. (Original work published 1966)

Hadley, H. L., & Fassbender, W. J. (2020). Recognizing religious identity in preservice teachers. In M. Juzwik, D. Davila, J. Stone, & K. Burke (Eds.), *Christian religious literacies: Histories, implications and alternative readings* (pp. 37–50).

Homer. (1919). *The odyssey.* Heinemann. doi:10.1177/1077800403259491

Laclau, E. (1995). Discourse. In R. E. Goodin & P. Pettit (Eds.), *A companion to contemporary political philosophy* (pp. 541–547). Blackwell.

Lather, P. (2004). Applied Derrida: (Mis)Reading the work of mourning in educational research. In P. P. Trifonas & M. A. Peters (Eds.), *Derrida, deconstruction and education: Ethics of pedagogy and research* (pp. 3–16). Blackwell.

Miedema, S., & Biesta, G. (2004). Jacques Derrida's religion with/out religion and the impossibility of religious education. *Religious Education, 99*(1), 23–37.

Montefiore, A. (2001). Talking liberties: Jacques Derrida's interview with Alan Montefiore. In G. J. Biesta & D. Egea-Kuehne (Eds.), *Derrida & education* (pp. 176–185). Routledge.

Philips, L., & Jorgensen, M. (2002). *Discourse analysis as theory and method.* SAGE Publications.

Sinha, S. (2013). Derrida, friendship and responsible teaching in contrast to effective teaching. *Educational Philosophy and Theory, 45*(3), 259–271.

CHAPTER THREE

In the Spirit of Inquiry: Portraiture

THE GUIDING METHODOLOGICAL FRAMEWORK for this study is portraiture—but a version of portraiture that is informed by poststructural and postmodern conceptions of identity, ethics, art, and science. This chapter offers a brief overview of how I conceptualize a Derridean-theorized portraiture. I then give a brief overview of my study participants and their school contexts (although this is more closely attended to in the portraits themselves). Finally, I outline the methodological argument for and process of the data collection, data analysis, and data representation for this study.

Traditional Portraiture Methodology

Portraiture is a qualitative research methodology that attempts to blend research with aesthetic representation to produce a research-based portrait that is accessible and useful to researchers and a wider audience. Portraiture situates research as "creative, subjective *and* rigorous" (Dixson, 2005, p. 107) and methodologically draws from the ethnographic tradition, privileging data collection through observation and interviews. Portraiture is a methodology that has its roots in educational research but has also been used in fields such as anthropology, psychology, sociology, and the humanities (Anderson, 2011; Ballengee-Morris, 2002; Shavarini, 2006; Stewart, 2002). In educational research, critical race theorists particularly have seen an overlap between the goals and purposes of critical race theory (CRT) and portraiture (Carter, 2003; Chapman, 2007; Dixson et al., 2005).

Sara Lawrence-Lightfoot, who is largely credited for creating and conceptualizing portraiture, draws her inspiration for the methodology of portraiture from her experience sitting for portraits. She describes the experience as "a dialogue between the portraitist and the subject" (Lawrence-Lightfoot & Davis, 1997, p. 3) that allows subjects "to feel *seen* . . . fully attended to, recognized, appreciated, respected, scrutinized" (p. 5) as they participate in a process committed to generous discovery and methodical investigation. The name itself, portraiture, is a metaphor for the kind of detail and representation that the researcher is aiming to achieve in the final product, but the portraiture metaphor also extends to the portraitist's stance toward the subjects of the portrait. A portrait, as Lawrence-Lightfoot and Davis (1997) point out, is a recognizable likeness of a real person. However, the artist or portraitist employs various artistic techniques—light and line, symbols and metaphor—to render the portrait as *more* than just a likeness of a person. Just like a portrait, the finished product is both representative and interpretive—capturing a truth or portraying *a* moment while still leaving space for various interpretations from the intended audience.

Like all methodologies, portraiture has very specific goals, affordances, and constraints. Portraiture draws heavily from ethnographic traditions. However, portraiture is unique in several important ways. First, one of the most distinguishing features of portraiture is its mandated and explicit focus on finding "goodness" in subjects and research contexts, a focus that, according to Lawrence-Lightfoot, is a direct reaction against research traditions that encourage identifications of problems from a deficit perspective. Second, portraiture doesn't just acknowledge the researcher's subjectivity and voice—it embraces it. The researcher's perspective is laid bare and celebrated in every aspect of the research project. Third, portraiture specifically is meant to engage a wider audience beyond academia through the researcher's careful attention to the aesthetic presentation of the data.

Goodness

Of all the characteristics of portraiture, the focus on "goodness" is most central to the present study and requires more explanation to make plain the goals and assumptions of my stance toward study participants. Portraiture's focus on what Lawrence-Lightfoot and Davis (1997) call "goodness" distinguishes it from many other kinds of research. Because *goodness* is a value-laden and extremely subjective term, it may be impossible to reach a standardized definition of what it means in every portraiture study. However, any working definition of the kind of goodness that portraiture is seeking to portray must define goodness contextually and with complication. That is, the portraitist is meant to understand how "goodness" is defined by the subjects in the setting and to portray multiple conceptions of "goodness." The portraitist "does not assume that there is a singular definition [of goodness] shared by all" (Lawrence-Lightfoot & Davis, 1997, p. 9). Goodness can mean different things in different settings, and the portraitist's job is to explain fully how and why goodness is defined in certain ways to certain subjects. Chapman (2005) explains that in educational research this search for goodness "highlights those habits and contributors to the ethos of the site that are affective mechanisms for promoting learning" (p. 28) In short, portraitists consciously are looking for strengths—in individuals, in research sites, and in institutions.

This focus on goodness does not mean that portraitists are looking to create flat heroes. Instead, portraitists are interested in complex concepts of goodness, which attend to strengths *and* weaknesses, identify promising practices *and* constraining practices, and celebrate empowerment while examining vulnerability. As Lawrence-Lightfoot and Davis (1997) point out, the portraitist assumes that "strength, health, and productivity . . . will *always* be imbued with flaws, weaknesses, and inconsistencies, and that the portraitist's inquiry must leave room for the full range of qualities to be revealed" (p. 142). The search for goodness does not just emerge as a category in data analysis or as a brief write-up in the final product. Instead, goodness is also conceptualized as the stance that the researcher or portraitist takes toward her own relationships with the subjects whom she wishes to portray. It is a very particular ethical stance that guides the work of a portraitist, a stance Lawrence-Lightfoot and Davis call both "generous *and* critical" (1997, p. 143).

The conception of "goodness" in portraiture has guided this study in various ways: First, engaging with portraiture has required me to consider my own definition of *goodness* (in teachers, in students, in educational systems) and consider how it converges and diverges with the definitions of *goodness* of my participants. Often, these areas of divergence were places where I encountered my own moments of hesitation as a researcher. Attending to both goodness and my own hesitations around these tensions allowed me to complicate the representation of the data and deepen my analysis of the participants and their educational practice. Second, the conception of goodness has influenced my stance toward research participants by inviting me to fully engage with the tension of what it means to responsibly construct and represent my participants while still leaving room for multiple representations that are simultaneously critical, generous, vulnerable, and productive.

The active role of the researcher in portraiture has led to some of its sharpest critiques. English (2000), for example, argued that

> what remains shrouded in portraiture is *the politics of vision*, that is, the uncontested right of the portraitist/researcher to situate, center, label, and fix in the tinctured hues of verbal descriptive prose what is professed to be 'real.' Admitting that such an activity is 'subjective' does not come close to dealing with the power to engage in it. (p. 21, emphasis original)

English is correct that the portraitist's active role leads to a great deal of subjectivity in interpretation, but portraiture, more than most qualitative approaches, attempts to lay bare *the politics of vision* of the researcher. Portraiture lays bare *the politics of vision* not by attempting to expunge the voice of the researcher to give a false veneer of impartiality or reliability but by fully acknowledging the partiality of the representations that are created throughout the portrait process (Gaztambide-Fernandez et al., 2011). Dixson et al. (2005) argue that this very partiality "provides the portraitist the space to acknowledge his or her presence . . . thereby dismantling the notion that the researcher is the only knower and expert on the lives and experiences of the participants" (p. 19). The portraitist uses her voice in the final research product to make plain all the ways that the portrait is a product of a subjective and partially representative research process. This portrait of evangelical teachers is no different: In my representation of my participants and their schools and classes, I am constantly present. Readers should take care to consider how these portraits might be different if done by another portraitist or researcher or if another research approach were used.

Audience

Portraiture is intended to be a rigorous research methodology, but it is also intended to create research products that are written for nonacademic audiences. Just like a painted portrait is an aesthetic representation of a person or a moment generally intended for wider audiences than just fellow artists, portraiture as a research methodology has the intent of making research accessible to audiences beyond fellow researchers. As Lawrence-Lightfoot (2005) says of recent shifts to participatory, relational, collaborative, and symmetric research,

> many of us are wanting to expand our audiences and welcome more voices into the public dialogues about education and schooling. If we want to broaden the audience for our work, then we must begin to speak in a language that is understandable, not exclusive and esoteric . . . a language that encourages identification, provokes debate, and invites reflection and action. But it is not only the language and idiom of our texts that will change, it is also that in anticipating different consumers of our work, we will begin to conceive of our research (the questions and design) differently from the very beginning. (p. 9)

Because the goal is accessibility, portraiture attends to aesthetic, audience, and *how* the research product is written, perhaps more consciously than other ethnographic methodologies. Even if a broader audience remains an aspirational goal for portraitist-researchers—as I think it does—I found value in pushing against emotionless (or a pretense of emotionless) and dry representations of research participants in that it allowed me to make clear my own experiences and emotional responses to participants and their stories.

Obviously, in portraiture, the portraitist makes many choices that shape interpretations, including whose voices are shared as well as what details are included or ignored. We might, of course, here think of the portraitist as a Derridean host who determines the limits of to whom the hospitality is offered and for how long, but we might also think, then, of the audience of the portrait as host*ed*—those others who are free to ask different questions, to challenge the host's interpretations of the world, to shake up the prevalent understandings of how things work by bringing new ways of being and seeing to the portraits. Bloom and Erlandson (2003), for example, conducted a study of different readers' varying interpretations of the same portraits. From this work, they concluded that it is "in the powerful, subjective interpretations that make a portrait more than a vita or a reference letter, [that] the balance of power between portraitist and reader is more evenly distributed" (Bloom & Erlandson, 2003, p. 891). The audience members, then, are situated as not just passive receptacles for the portraitist's interpretations and viewpoints but as active participants in meaning-making as well. Portraiture as a methodology, then, invites your participation as a reader to make meaning alongside me as the portraitist, to see things differently, or to call into question my reliability as a portraitist.

Poststructural Portraiture and Adaptations for This Study

Portraiture is particularly well suited for exploring counternarratives, a project that has often been aligned closely with critical theories such as CRT, critical feminist theories, and Marxist theories (among many others). But how might portraiture interact with a poststructural theoretical framework? Is it possible to construct a poststructural portrait? Poststructural scholars use portraiture and other ethnographic methodologies but are aware of the inherent tensions between ethnographic methodological assertions of truth and reality with poststructural contestations over the slippery nature of language and the constitution of selfhood.

Briefly (and far too simply), poststructuralism questions what seems commonsensical, considering instead what discursive conditions exist to make certain ways of knowing knowable and certain ways of being possible (Foucault, 1966/1971). That is, poststructuralism is less concerned with finding "truth" and more concerned with studying discursive practices to explore how humans produce contextual meanings of truth (Bové, 1990; St Pierre, 2000). In this way, language is seen as productive in that language creates the subject of which it speaks, but language is never able to represent reality in that words only have meaning within cultural narratives. The meaning of words is also always already deferred, as language is constantly changing and taking on new meanings (Derrida, 1978).

Portraiture, on the other hand, attempts to portray reality. While it is acknowledged that the researcher is constructing their own version of reality, an assumption of portraiture is that there *is* a reality to be captured (even if it is a fleeting reality) and that the portraitist's goal is to approximate that reality as closely as possible through an aesthetic representation of data. Additionally, portraiture has an assumption of identity that is singular and stable—at least in the moment of portraiture—which is, perhaps, one of the reasons why portraiture has been so successfully used in studies that center identity and view power as a have/have-not dichotomy (e.g., studies informed by CRT; see Carter, 2003; Chapman, 2007; Dixson et al., 2005, for examples). My analysis of the commensurability of portraiture with poststructural theories does not attempt to minimize the tensions inherent here; rather, I consider the axiological alignment between the ethics of Derrida and the purpose of portraiture and attend to ways in which portraiture might hold space for poststructuralist conceptions of research and science.

Commensurability and Axiology

One of the most compelling arguments for the commensurability of poststructural theories with a methodology most closely aligned with critical and constructivist paradigms is a careful examination of the axiology of both the theory and the methodology. Lincoln and colleagues (2011) assert that arguing over whether paradigms are commensurable "is probably less useful than to probe where and how paradigms exhibit confluence and where and how they exhibit differences, controversies, and contradictions" (p. 97). Particularly, they argue that it is possible to blend paradigmatic elements "if the models share axiomatic elements that are similar or that resonate strongly" (Lincoln et al., 2011, p. 117). Lincoln et al. position the axiology of a paradigm (defined as the branch of philosophy dealing with ethics, aesthetics, and religion) as equally important as the epistemology or ontology of the paradigm; in matters of commensurability, they argue it is *the* most important factor. They argue that expanding conversations of paradigmatic modes of inquiry to include axiology is one way that qualitative research might achieve greater confluence between various paradigms and inquiry models.

The question, then, of whether portraiture is commensurable with Derridean ethics has less to do with whether conceptions of knowledge, or reality and existence are similar enough and more to do with whether the axiological approach of portraiture is commensurable with the axiology of Derrida's conception of hospitality, otherness, and ethical decision-making. Are the ethical purpose and goal of portraiture at odds with Derridean ethics? Lawrence-Lightfoot and Davis (1997) make clear that one of the primary purposes of portraiture is to open a new relationship between researcher and participants—one in which the participants "feel *seen* . . . fully attended to, recognized, appreciated, respected, scrutinized" (p. 5) as they participate in a process committed to generous discovery and methodical investigation. Compare this with Derrida's conception of the deconstruction of the subject, which invites an affirmation of difference while still saying, "*Yes*, I *speak* to you, I *address* you, I *listen* to you" (Derrida, 2001, p. 180). Derrida and Lawrence-Lightfoot and Davis, then, share a sense of ethics—an axiological approach—to others and otherness.

Holding Space

It is not just a conception of responsibility to others that has been important in guiding my selection of portraiture as a methodology. In several ways, portraiture holds space for other paradigmatic tensions between poststructural theories and more traditional research models. As Britzman (2003) points out, ethnography and ethnographic-influenced methodologies like portraiture are a "regulating fiction" (p. 253) that produce their own version of truth, identity, and power relationship. If this tension of production, construction, and representation within regulating discursive structures is to be worked to effect in ethnographic (or portraiture) studies, then Britzman argues for a new kind of ethnography that does more complicated work and has more complex goals than a simple or straightforward representation of reality:

> The reason we might read and do ethnography [or portraiture], then, is to think the unthought in more complex ways, to trouble confidence in being able to observe behavior, apply the correct technique, and correct what is taken as a mistake. Ethnographic narratives should trace how power circulates and surprises, theorize how subjects spring from the discourses that incite them, and question the belief in representation even as one must practice representation as a way to intervene critically in the constitutive constraints of discourses. (2003, p. 253)

Some aspects of portraiture open up and hold space for the kinds of ethnographic goals Britzman suggests. For example, portraiture's insistence on deep contextualization of both the ethnographer/portraitist and the subject of the portrait allows for complicated narratives about subjectivity and discourse, including an open discussion of power circulation between the portraitist and the subject. Portraiture is, in some regards, born out of the poststructural move to push against structural binaries that place art and science as opposites. Instead, portraiture encourages the boundary crossing of representation and the bricolage of flexible and creative thinking that might allow for a complex, explicitly partial, and nuanced representation of the subject of the portrait in a way that attends openly to the tensions Britzman describes.

Research Participants and Contexts

This section is intended as a broad overview of the participants of the study and of the school contexts in which they teach (more specifics about each participant and their school contexts can be found in their portraits, in Part II).

The three participants in this study were selected from the participants in a previous study that I had previously been a part of that examined the experiences of evangelical preservice teachers in an English education teacher preparation program. Because I wanted to create more lengthy and complex portraits of participants, I studied three participants, all of whom were former students in classes I taught as part of that program. I purposefully selected former students as participants because of the personal nature of my research topic—in the hopes that our previous relationship might have already built in a certain amount of trust and openness as I asked them to talk about sensitive matters like belief and religious practice. Additionally, all the participants identified themselves as evangelical Christians and were in their first 3 years of teaching in a public school setting during the study period.

The three participants[1] also represent a variety of teaching experiences and classroom contexts. Mallory and Mei teach high school while Noelle teaches middle school. While Mallory teaches 11th-grade English, Mei teaches sheltered language arts courses for English for Speakers of Other Languages. Noelle has a dual certification in language arts and social sciences and teaches a composite humanities course at a public STEAM (science, technology, engineering, arts, and medicine)–focused middle school. The participants are also in various stages of being new teachers: Noelle is a first-year teacher, Mallory is a second-year teacher, and Mei is a third-year teacher.

Table 3.1: *Participant Information*

	Noelle Andrews	Mei Lin	Mallory Donaldson
School	Roosevelt Middle School	Oakcrest High School	Short Creek High School
Teaching Assignment	7th-grade humanities (ELA and social studies)	11th- and 12th-grade English (with ESOL students)	11th-grade English (On-level and Honors)
Gender	Female	Female	Female
Race/Ethnicity	White	Chinese	White
Years of Teaching Experience	1	3	2
Religious Affiliation	Presbyterian Church of America (as a child) Reformed Baptist (currently)	Nondenominational Chinese and Chinese American church (Reformed)	Non-denominational megachurch (leans Baptist)

Note. ELA = English language arts; ESOL = English for Speakers of Other Languages.

The three participants all teach in the same school district, although they teach at different schools. I include here general data on each teacher's school context for reference.

Table 3.2: *School Contexts*

	Noelle Andrews	Mei Lin	Mallory Donaldson
School	Roosevelt Middle School	Oakcrest High School	Short Creek High School
Grades	6–8	9–12	9–12
Enrollment	~800	~3,800	~3,100
Student Race/ Ethnicity	37% Black 21% Hispanic 19% White 18% Asian/Pacific Islander 6% Multiracial	48% Hispanic 28% Black 14% White 7% Asian/Pacific Islander 3% Multiracial	29% Black 27% Hispanic 26% White 13% Asian/Pacific Islander 5% Multiracial

Data Collection

I used ethnographic data collection methods such as interviews, observations, and document and artifact collection. I collected (and began early analysis of) data in a variety of ways over 9 weeks. The primary sources of data were individual interviews and focus groups with all the participants. Supplementary data from participants' self-reflective videos, photos of teachers' classrooms, and written blogs and responses were equally helpful in creating a more complicated portrait of each participant. The first data collection point was a focus group meeting where participants were introduced to the Derridean aporias of ethics that would frame their definition of a moment of hesitation. In this meeting, participants also shared their initial noticings about classroom decisions that caused them to feel a moment of hesitation specifically because they were an evangelical Christian teacher.

Following the first focus group, each participant had three one-on-one semistructured interviews with me (see Table 3.3 for the structured questions for each interview and focus group). The first interview focused on participants' religious beliefs and backgrounds, the second interview guided participants in unpacking their self-reported moments of hesitation using Derridean ethics as a framework, and the third interview focused on teachers' beliefs and practices around teaching. Additionally, as a part of the first interview, participants gave me a tour of their classroom, and I photographed artifacts in their rooms, which were of particular interest to the study, reflected the personality of the participant, or highlighted the participant's teaching practice. Between interviews, participants agreed to reflect (either in a blog or through a video reflection) on any moments of hesitation that they experienced around their religious identity in their classroom. All participants met again as part of a final focus group, which served as a group debriefing of the participants' moments of hesitation. In this focus group, I also asked participants to reflect on the benefits and drawbacks of participating in the study.

After each portrait was written, each participant member-checked their portrait through email exchanges with me, correcting details that I had gotten wrong or clarifying what they had meant or said in a particular moment. Participants were given a gift card at the completion of the study as an acknowledgment of the time they spent as part of the research process.

Table 3.3: *Focus Group and Interview Questions*

Focus Group 1—Introduce "Moments of Hesitation" terminology; discuss Derridean ethics; initial exploration of moments of hesitation
What are some of your experiences that you'd be willing to share with the group, from your teaching so far that would fit the definition of a moment of hesitation?
What tensions are you aware of between your identity as a Christian and your identity as a teacher?
Where do you experience these tensions?
When do you experience these tensions?
Why do you experience these tensions?
Interview 1—Religious background and current belief
What denomination did you grow up in? Do you still identify with that denomination?
What are the characteristics of that denomination?
Would you use the term evangelical to describe yourself? Why/why not?
Would you use the term fundamentalist to describe yourself? Why/why not?
Would you use the term charismatic to describe your church? Why/why not?
What are your beliefs about God? Who is God? What are the characteristics of God?
What is your conception about God's will and free choice?
What is your conception of God's love?
What were you taught it means to show God's love? What does that look like? (As a teacher?)
What do you believe is your responsibility as a Christian in this life?
How do you manifest that responsibility?
In your church, how should children act around adults? What is the conception of adult authority?
What is the responsibility of adults to children and teens in your church?
What is your conception of grace? (As a teacher?)
What is the role of women in your church?
What are your conceptions of heaven/hell?
Can you define sin for me? What is sin? What happens when you sin? How do you avoid or overcome sin?
Do you believe you can live a perfect life? Why/why not?
Do you feel like you struggle with perfectionism? Why or why not? Is that tied in any way to your religious belief?
What does it mean to follow Christ's example as a teacher?
Who was Christ as a teacher? What does his example of teaching mean for you as a teacher?
Did you feel called to teaching? When?
What did that calling look/feel like?
Do you see the work of an ELA teacher as manifesting God's will? In what ways? Why/why not?
Interview 2—Reviewing moments of hesitation (For this interview, I brought a summary of the moments of hesitation that each participant had talked about in their blog or Flipgrid reflections and asked them to unpack each moment of hesitation using Derrida's identification of the aporias of ethical decision making.)
What's the context of this decision? What made it a difficult choice? What tensions were you feeling in that moment?
What was the pull of the tensions? Like, who were you aware that you were being responsible or irresponsible to in that moment? Was your own comfort an issue in that moment?
What did you decide to do? How did you deal with it? What was the outcome? How did you feel about your decision?

Interview 3—Teacher beliefs and practice
Can you tell me what kind of student you are most drawn to or connect most easily with? Can you tell me what kind of student you most struggle to connect with? How would a student know that you really connect with them or care for them? How would a student know that you are struggling to connect with them? What is your definition of a good teacher? What is your definition of good instruction? What is your definition of good assessment? What is your definition of a good student? Has teaching been what you thought it would be? What has surprised you for better? What has surprised you for worse? How do you navigate that mismatch between expectation and reality? Can you tell me about a time when you had a disciplinary exchange or a corrective interaction with a student that you're proud of the way that you handled it? What happened? Why are you proud of the way you handled it? What values of yours as a teacher does it reflect? Why are those values important to you? Can you tell me about a time when you had a disciplinary exchange or a corrective interaction with a student that you regret? What happened? Why do you regret the way you handled it? What values of yours did you not attend to? Can you tell me about a lesson plan or a unit that you created this year that you are most proud of? What values of yours does it attend to? Can you tell me about a lesson plan or unit that you felt was less successful? What didn't you like about it? How would you change it in the future? Can you tell me about an assessment (either formative or summative) that you created that reflects your values as a teacher? Can you tell me about an assessment that your kids experience (either formative or summative and it doesn't HAVE to be created by you) that DOESN'T reflect your values as a teacher?
Focus Group 2—Group debrief of common moments of hesitation and interview experience
Have you found any benefits to having participated in this study? Have there been any drawbacks to having participated in this study? What moments of hesitation are you more aware of now that you have completed this research? How do you think your religious identity is affecting your classroom practice? Is there any moment of hesitation that you would like to debrief with the group?

Note. ELA = English language arts.

I was guided by traditional portraiture methods of interviewing, observation, and multiple data sources. What I found, however, was that in a poststructural portraiture like this one, data are not easily bounded by formalized data collection procedures. Although my official institutional review board–approved data collection consists of interviews, a collection of photos of teachers' classrooms, focus groups, and self-reflection videos, it would be disingenuous to say those data pieces are the only data on which I have drawn as I have created portraits of my participants. For example, all the participants have been students in a teacher preparation classroom I have taught. It would be impossible for me to cut out of my data collection, analysis, and representation the things I know about them and from them in that context. I am "friends" with all the participants on social media sites and in real life. I have written letters of recommendation for two of the three participants. There are several moments in the audio recordings in which a participant discloses something to me and I turn off the recording to protect their emotional response and privacy (e.g., I conducted an interview with Noelle 3 days after her breakup with her long-term boyfriend, and her emotion over that spilled into our discussion). I do, however, still consider these unrecorded moments and interactions as data that help shape my portraits of each participant. In short, those experiences cannot help but color and shape my understanding of the participants, their classroom environments, their religious beliefs, and their classroom practice.

Data Analysis

Portraitists view data analysis as an iterative process and value flexible systems of data organization, analysis, and synthesis. Lawrence-Lightfoot and Davis (1997) suggest that one helpful tool for a portraitist might be Glaser and Strauss's (1967) "constant comparative method," where much of the synthesis, analysis, and reflection of the data happens throughout the research project instead of at the end. However, Lawrence-Lightfoot and Davis refrain from prescribing set coding methods or giving strict analytical guidance. Instead, they urge portraitists to be reflective and thorough in their consideration of collected data, not only allowing time for daily reflections but also allowing for post–data collection analysis that "is less action-oriented and more ruminative" (Lawrence-Lightfoot & Davis, 1997, p. 189). For this study, I regularly wrote (once every 3 to 5 days) during the data collection and analysis process to build in space for this kind of ruminative analysis.

I also passed through the collected data multiple times to identify regularities and patterns to guide the final representation of each portrait, looking carefully for symbols that might shape the narrative. Each reading offered "the opportunity of listening for a 'different voice,' from a different angle, and with an ear to the subtle meanings and complex perspectives" (Lawrence-Lightfoot & Davis, 1997, p. 191). For these readings and for the majority of the analysis, I worked to make sure that I did not decontextualize the data I had collected. Because portraiture (and, even more so, poststructural portraiture) is driven by highly contextualized and localized portraits of people and institutions, separating participants' responses and reflections into small chunks for analysis would be counterintuitive to the process (Maxwell, 2013).

For this study, I analyzed the data by paying close attention to the following five modes of synthesis that Lawrence-Lightfoot and Davis (1997) identify as essential to a portraiture study: (1) repetitive refrains that collectively express common beliefs or viewpoints; (2) resonant metaphors that the subjects of the portrait themselves use to describe their experiences; (3) institutional and cultural rituals that reveal values and priorities of the participants; (4) attention to multiple sources of data, interview data, observation data, factual data that provide context for the research question; and (5) convergent voices and patterns. To account for these, I made five distinct passes through the collected data to attend to each of these areas of synthesis. All this reflective analysis was done with the goal of rigorous but flexible examination and interpretation that allows for a representation of complexity in research sites and subjects.

Data Representation

Once the data had been collected and analyzed, I turned my attention to representing it as a complete portrait or an aesthetic whole, in Lawrence-Lightfoot's words. In truth, for this poststructural portrait, I worked to create a complete portrait, but I also worked to create splintered and multiple portraits that attend to multiplicity and non-unity in each subject. In representing the data, the portraitist grapples with all "the tensions inherent in blending art and science, analysis and narrative, description and interpretation, structure and texture" (Lawrence-Lightfoot & Davis, 1997, p. 243). My goal in the representational choices that I made was to create an artistic written portrait that aesthetically expresses the inquiry process and data collection with rich detail.

The representation of data in a traditional portraiture study is a single narrative that carefully weaves together rigorous data collection from interviews, observations, and written data sources, with artistic expression, using literary techniques such as metaphor, foreshadowing, symbolism, and voice into an aesthetic whole. The final portrait provides rich context about the people and institutions it represents and gives complex, layered, and nuanced representations that both answer the research questions and leave possibilities for new questions, new interpretations, and new representations. As I wrote the portraits of my participants, I attempted to tease out how portraiture methodology might be modified to account for poststructural conceptions of identity, language, and representation. What this means in practical terms is that I am not attempting to create a "whole portrait" or a "complete picture" of my participants. Instead, I create portraits of each participant using narratives that are inherently multiple, purposefully slivered into liminal moments that allow space for contradiction in identity, in practice, and in responses.

As I began to work with the representation of the data, I found that there were several liminal moments in my interactions with the participants that stymied me in terms of representation. While I could create a narrative that accounted for the factual details of these moments, I was left deeply dissatisfied by these narratives. I felt that I was either providing too little information to accurately capture the emotions of these moments or that the real power of these moments occurred because of the interaction of my own emotional response to what participants were saying—even when that emotion wasn't visible in the interview data or observation notes. Instead, to represent these liminal moments, I have turned to a poetic representation. In creating these poems, I draw heavily on the work of Freeman (2017), who argues that poetical thinking and poetical representations are not necessarily about art but are instead about "unleashing our perceptual, aesthetical capacities for sensual knowing" (p. 72) with an aim to "bring into being the complexities of sensed experiences" (p. 73). Freeman argues that poetic inquiry is less an *interpretation* and more an *invitation* for others to enter the "world of human experience" (2017, p. 79). For the most complex interactions between myself and my research participants, I use poetry not to *explain* or *represent* the facts of the interactions but, instead, to invite readers to the perceptual experience of these interactions.

For a poststructural portraiture study like this one, this kind of poetical thinking and representation works to hold space for poststructural conceptions of language and multiplicity and further invites a complicated exploration of the ethics of representation. Freeman (2017) states that poetical inquiry "makes full use of the ontological, generative space of becoming" (p. 79) by privileging language's performative and figurative functions instead of literal and representational functions. The focus in poetical inquiry on language as pliable, emotive, and fluid holds space for Derridean conceptions of language as slippery and always and already deferring meaning. According to Freeman, poetical inquiry "seeks to engage while also shocking us out of our complacency, keeping images and words from ever becoming fixed" (2017, p. 81)—attuning itself to poststructural conceptions of language that make space for a deconstruction of the political, theological, and socioeconomic commitments of words. In turn, this centering of language as pliable, performative, and figurative opens up multiple interpretations of the inquiry process and its representation of participant identity—a key feature of postmodern portraiture in visual arts and a characteristic of this particular poststructural postmodern research project.

Note

1. The names of all participants, schools, and students mentioned in portraits have been assigned pseudonyms.

References

Anderson, L. M. (2011). Toward professional integration in the humanities: One teacher-researcher's experience with portraiture. *Arts & Humanities in Higher Education, 10*(1), 103–119.

Ballengee-Morris, C. (2002). Cultures for sale: Perspectives on colonialism and self-determination and the relationship to authenticity and tourism. *Studies in Art Education, 43*(3), 232–245.

Bloom, C. M., & Erlandson, D. A. (2003). Three voices in portraiture: Actor, artist, and audience. *Qualitative Inquiry, 9*(6), 874–894.

Bové, P. A. (1990). Discourse. In F. Lentricchia & T. McLaughlin (Eds.), *Critical terms for literary study* (pp. 50–65). University of Chicago Press.

Britzman, D. P. (2003). *Practice makes practice: A critical study of learning to teach* (Rev. ed.). State University of New York Press.

Carter, M. (2003). Telling tales out of school: "What's the fate of a Black story in a White world of White stories?" In G. R. Lopez & L. Parker (Eds.), *Interrogating racism in qualitative research methodology* (pp. 28–48). Peter Lang.

Chapman, T. K. (2005). Expressions of "voice" in portraiture. *Qualitative Inquiry, 11*(1), 27–51.

Chapman, T. K. (2007). Interrogating classroom relationships and events: Using portraiture and critical race theory in education research. *Educational Researcher, 36*(3), 156–162.

Derrida, J. (2001). Talking liberties: Jacques Derrida's interview with Alan Montefiore. In G. Biesta & D. Egea-Kuehne (Eds.), *Derrida & Education* (pp. 176–185). Routledge.

Derrida, J. (1978). Structure, sign and play in the discourse of the human sciences. In Jacques Derrida, *Writing and difference* (A. Bass, Trans.; pp. 278–293). The University of Chicago Press.

Dixson, A. D. (2005). Extending the metaphor: Notions of jazz in portraiture. *Qualitative Inquiry, 11*(1), 106–137.

Dixson, A. D., Chapman, T. K., & Hill, D. A. (2005). Research as an aesthetic process: Extending the portraiture methodology. *Qualitative Inquiry, 11*(1), 16–26.

English, F. W. (2000). A critical appraisal of Sara Lawrence-Lightfoot's *portraiture* as a method of educational research. *Educational Researcher, 29*(7), 21–26.

Foucault, M. (1971). *The order of things: An archaeology of the human sciences.* Vintage. (Original work published 1966)

Freeman, M. (2017). *Modes of thinking for qualitative data analysis.* Routledge.

Gaztambide-Fernandez, R., Cairns, K., Kawashima, Y., Menna, L., & VanderDussen, E. (2011). Portraiture as pedagogy: Learning research through the exploration of context and methodology. *International Journal of Education and the Arts, 12*(4). http://www.ijea.org/v12n4/

Glaser, B. G., & Straus, A. S. (1967). *The discovery of grounded theory: Strategies for qualitative research.* Aldine De Gruyter.

Lawrence-Lightfoot, S. (2005). Reflections on portraiture: A dialogue between art and science. *Qualitative Inquiry, 11*(1), 3–15.

Lawrence-Lightfoot, S., & Davis, J. H. (1997). *The art and science of portraiture.* Jossey-Bass.

Lincoln, Y. S., Lynham, S. A., & Guba, E. G. (2011). Paradigmatic controversies, contradictions, and emerging confluences, revisited. In N. K. Denzin & Y. S. Lincoln (Eds.), *The SAGE handbook of qualitative research* (4th ed., pp. 97-128). SAGE Publications.

Maxwell, M. A. (2013). *Qualitative research design: An interactive approach* (3rd ed.). SAGE Publications.

Shavarini, M. (2006). The role of higher education in the life of a young Iranian woman. *Women's Studies International Quarterly, 29*(1), 42–53.

St. Pierre, E. A. (2000). Poststructural feminism in education: An overview. *International Journal of Qualitative Studies in Education, 13*(5), 477–515.

Stewart, D. (2002). The role of faith in the development of an integrated identity: A qualitative study of Black students at a White college. *Journal of College Student Development, 43*(4), 579–596.

PART II

Individual Portraits

DEBORAH BRITZMAN'S (2003) INFLUENTIAL study of English teachers' practice and preparation draws on Willard Waller's work (1961) to engage with "one of the most provocative questions in the research on teaching . . . 'What does teaching do to teachers?'" (p. 25). This question opens up a line of inquiry for Britzman into the private struggles of the teaching profession, an inquiry that allows researchers to "uncover the dynamics, tensions, exclusions, and inclusions" (2003, p. 25) engendered by the activity of teaching. The portraits of individual teachers that follow are very much asking a similar question for a similar purpose.

Each of the following three chapters examines the beliefs, experiences, and practices of new English language arts teachers at an early stage in their career as they work to make sense of their school contexts, their teaching philosophies and practices, and their interactions with the youth in their classrooms. They were kind (and brave) enough to share ethically complicated situations that they encountered in their classrooms, even when those situations left them feeling unsure of whether they did "the right thing." From our conversations, I have created a portrait of each teacher that emphasizes the places where their teacher identity feels pulled, fractured, and tentative. To think through Waller's question of what teaching does to teachers, I have also emphasized the places where the teachers' religious identities also were stretched or altered by the demands of teaching. These are sometimes painful and always personal portraits that inquire into the specific "dynamics, tensions, exclusions, and inclusions" (Britzman, 2003, p. 25) engendered by teachers who identify themselves as evangelical Christians.

The value of considering such a question—what teaching does to teachers?—is that it makes space for an examination of the subjectivities of teachers. Britzman (2003) says that an examination of teacher experience, identity, and subjectivity reveals a "concern with *how* the activity of teaching expresses something about the subjectivities of the teachers and determines ways teachers come to construct their teaching identities" (p. 25). These kinds of inquiry make space for complex understandings of teachers and teacher identities.

However, these portraits—as generously as they are written, as sympathetic as they are to the complex demands on new teachers' religious and school identities—exist to very specifically examine the intentional and unintentional exclusions and inclusions that teacher identities and subjectivities bring into being. Returning to Derrida, although the ultimate goal of school and classroom hospitality is an unconditional welcome for every student and teacher, these portraits work to point out the current limitations of hospitality and to point out most clearly who is included and excluded from being "the subject of his or her own experience, life, activity, responsibilities and so on" (Montefiore, 2001, p. 177).

It is worth noting, too, that as a portraitist, I am largely unconcerned with whether the participants are (in)correctly aligning their personal practice with the doctrines of their faith. I am much more interested in the ways teachers actually enact their religious identities than in examining whether that enactment comes from a misreading of scripture or a flawed understanding of their own beliefs. In our interviews, I chose to respect their definitions of their beliefs about God, faith, and evangelicism.

The following chapters are organized into two parts. The first part of each chapter is the portrait itself—the representation of the research. Each portrait is then followed by an examination of how the theoretical framework of Derridean hospitality and ethics deepens an understanding of how each teacher navigates the moments of hesitation that they encounter in the classroom.

References

Britzman, D. P. (2003). *Practice makes practice: A critical study of learning to teach* (Rev. ed.). State University of New York Press.

Montefiore, A. (2001). Talking liberties: Jacques Derrida's interview with Alan Montefiore. In G. J. Biesta & D. Egea-Kuehne (Eds.), *Derrida & education* (pp. 176–185). Routledge.

Waller, W. (1961). *The sociology of teaching.* Russell and Russell.

CHAPTER FOUR

Portraits of Noelle: Balancing Acts

NOELLE ANDREWS IS SPENDING a good portion of her first year of teaching seventh grade chasing a rabbit around her room. "That was a mistake," Noelle says with an eye roll. "I thought it would be fun to have a classroom pet, and I guess the kids love it. But it's a pain." The fluffy white bunny hops around the classroom during class, so much so that Noelle's had to institute a rule that no one can put food on the floor because her middle schoolers kept dropping food in the hope that the bunny would come sit by them. The bunny insists on roaming freely. If Noelle tries to cage him during a lesson, he loudly kicks up against the cage, over and over and over, until she lets him out. "I *should* have prayed about the rabbit," she says and laughs as she tells me that she doesn't believe in praying about every little thing, "because He would have said no."

Noelle spent the summer before her first year of teaching studying to pass the certification exam for social studies content so that she could teach humanities—a block-scheduled course that requires both language arts and social studies certifications. As an undergraduate, she studied English literature, but she returned to receive her initial certification in teaching through a master's in teaching program at the local university—which is how I met her as her Teaching Reading instructor. She's either a dark blonde or light brunette (depending on lighting) and petite, and it feels like her face exists almost wholly to frame her large, expressive blue eyes. When she was a student, I considered her to be serious and driven—the kind of student who reread the directions multiple times before turning assignments in to make sure she'd done everything correctly—but I discover in our interviews that she's also got a dry sense of humor. "I have a lot of moments of hesitation," she confesses wryly, "because I'm pretty bad at this. I'm just learning a lot as a first-year teacher."

Some of this, of course, is because the first year of teaching is hard. It's difficult to imagine Noelle raising her voice to get the students' attention. She has a low, sometimes gravelly voice and a sweet disposition, and she has suddenly found herself with a classroom full of loud, energetic, and sometimes frustrating seventh graders who get noisy. A lot. "Classroom management is hard for me," she says, "but I have a good time with my students." Noelle considers her job as a teacher to teach content, of course. But more important, she sees her job as an opportunity to exemplify mature adult behavior and provide steadiness and love for kids who may not always have something steady in their lives. A large part of Noelle's sense of teaching is informed by her sense of herself as a religious and spiritual person. In fact, her evangelical Christian identity makes her teacher identity possible. She states, "I don't think I would be a teacher if I wasn't a Christian" because it's an opportunity to teach kids—"to accept them, and love them, and show them kindness"—all values and ways of being that are deeply tied to Noelle's identity as a Christian. Teaching, loving, and accepting the kids in her classroom is the kind of evangelism that Noelle feels most comfortable with, and she confesses that she rarely feels like she needs to directly evangelize, although she answers honestly when kids ask her about her beliefs.

Listening to Noelle talk about her religious identity and her teaching identity, I can't help but think about how much of her approach as a religiously informed teacher is informed by a sense of balance. She is finely attuned to what she can and can't say (or perhaps, more accurately, what she will and won't say); she walks a tightrope constantly between how honest she is with her students and how much she shields them from the messy reality of life; she carefully considers what her classroom evangelism looks like and how it might be picked up by students.

Noelle Andrews is herself a product of a long tradition of balancing acts. Her parents are both African—White Africans, one from South Africa, one from Zimbabwe. They are *not* descendants of Christian missionaries, thank you very much, but "English peasants who went to [Africa to] work on the railroad." Although the majority of Noelle's childhood was spent in the United States, her African heritage is important to her, and she takes an active interest in the politics of Zimbabwe and South Africa. She sponsors a child's education through a Christian-affiliated education fund, something she shared with her class when they covered African current events as part of their curriculum. There are moments, too, when you can hear a colonial African influence in her speech, like when she says "boar-row" for *borrow*.

Noelle's religious belief is the product of deeply religious parents, although her parents were raised in very different denominations. Her parents' different religious upbringings have created an ability for Noelle to move between denominations with some amount of ease. There are a number of points of doctrine that she personally believes but would be uncomfortable insisting that everyone needed to believe to be saved, and I can't help but think that some of that is because her extended family and parents have embraced Christianity from a variety of viewpoints. Her father was raised as a Roman Catholic (the kind of Catholic, Noelle explains, who treasures a piece of carpet the pope once walked on), but he left Catholicism as a teenager—largely because he was "a social beast" and the evangelical churches had stronger youth groups where he could hang out during the week with his friends. Noelle's mother was raised in a very traditional Baptist church, something "she still very much claims." Noelle has attended a variety of churches: mostly Presbyterian Church of America (PCA; the more conservative Presbyterian branch) as a child and Baptist churches or Baptist-leaning nondenominational churches during her college years. Noelle's parents, too, tend to "flip-flop between PCA and Baptist churches" because her father likes the more traditional worship in the PCA, but the family aligns more closely with Baptist doctrine with regard to infant baptism.

Noelle freely admits that she has a perfectionistic streak—something that she views as both a gift and a problem. As a student, it meant that she had some of the highest grades in her cohort and received multiple scholarships. As a teacher, it means that she's always planning ahead and is well prepared for every class. She excels at the organizational routines that make up the behind-the-scenes majority of a teacher's job, but if she has to leave something undone, it gives her anxiety. She attributes some of her perfectionism to her father's more conservative, Catholic approach to religion. "My parents loved me," she says,

> but looking back, I can see that there were a lot of areas where I didn't give myself grace because it was like—you get it right or it's wrong. So I very much kind of see that influence in myself and I can see like my dad doing that to himself . . . that's kind of Catholic, like, it's works-based.

For Noelle, her inability to give herself grace and her need to perform perfectly has led to a great deal of educational success and has allowed her to make order out of the chaotic experience that is the first year of teaching. At the same time, she would like to be able to give herself grace as a reflection of a deeper trust in the grace of God.

Like most evangelicals, Noelle believes that she is saved in and through the grace of Jesus Christ. When I ask her what it means to be an evangelical (a term that she will readily use to identify herself), she says,

> For me, that means that I am Christian both in word and in practice, whereas I would use the word "nominal" [to describe] someone who identifies very loosely with believing in Jesus and God, but doesn't hold to any practices that influence the way they live their life on a daily basis.

Noelle's faith *does* influence her everyday practice. She attends church weekly, prays, reads the Bible, and tries to show God's love by "just being a good person who's happy and is generally edifying." Noelle's primary religious affiliation, PCA, is Calvinist in tradition, which means that Noelle believes that God ordained her belief and saved her because He chose to. God's ordination of her salvation has nothing to do with her own choices or free will.

Agency, foreordination, and predestination are key concepts for Noelle personally and for her denomination. When I ask her how a person might know if God has ordained their salvation,[1] she pauses for a minute to think about how she wants to phrase her response:

> I think it's probably a lot more complicated than this, but basically, if you are worried about being chosen and whether or not you can be saved and whether or not God is going to forgive you, you probably are [ordained for salvation], because that's not something you're going to question or be concerned about if you don't have some kind of innate desire to have that which you would only have from God.

Noelle's religious beliefs are marked by clear delineations and binaries—saved/not saved, heaven/hell, righteousness/sin, good/bad, true/false. God makes the positive side of all of these binaries possible and achievable for humankind. Men and women are fallen, innately sinful, constantly drawn to the negative side of each binary. "No person," Noelle tells me, "could of their complete own volition ever want to be saved by God. No one would run away from being sinful and selfish without God having planted the desire in them." For Noelle, every selfless act is a result of God's call to obedience, and every selfish act is a showing forth of the inherent sinfulness within.

I ask Noelle why God chooses certain people to be saved, and she shrugs and says flatly, "I don't know." She pauses and adds more carefully, "I mean, I think God's love is all-encompassing, but being reformed[2] also complicates things because it's like God loves everybody, but not everybody loves God. Most people don't." This is a point of doctrine for Noelle that she personally believes in but that she admits to not fully understanding. She is bothered by the reformed evangelical community's preoccupation with convincing every other Christian that they must be reformed to be saved. Noelle believes strongly in reformation doctrines personally, but she doesn't think everyone who is a Christian needs to believe the exact same way. She divides beliefs into tiers—Tier 1 beliefs are core Christian principles that every Christian should hold—"Do you believe in God? Do you believe in Jesus? . . . Do you believe the Bible is true?" These are the questions that a Christian *must* be able to answer affirmatively to be, well, a Christian. But there are other theological questions that Noelle believes are interpretive, and these beliefs, which she calls Tier 2 or Tier 3 beliefs, she has little interest in arguing. She prefers a less fundamental, less legalistic approach to worship and belief because she believes that there can be a middle ground on many issues. Most important, she doesn't believe that her (or anyone's) salvation hinges on a perfect understanding of God—a stance that perhaps not only allows her to not think too much about why some people are elected and others aren't but also allows her to hold strong personal beliefs while still engaging with people who hold different beliefs without feeling an overwhelming need to evangelize.

Noelle's Calvinist-informed beliefs about God's sovereignty give her a great deal of comfort as a teacher and as a person. She believes that God's will is sovereign but that she has free choice within that sovereignty:

> God's will and what He has ordained is going to take place regardless of the decisions I make, but the means by which His will and His plan come to fruition can differ based on my decisions. God's not a computer. It's not like, okay, Noelle is supposed to do this one thing with her life, but she made a huge mistake and decided to be an English Education major . . . and now that she's done this her life is ruined. If you were to believe that people have that much power and their own free will, I would be terrified to ever do anything with my life! But because God is sovereign over my life and his plan, I can live without fear of making a huge mistake. I don't have that much power, I guess.

For Noelle, her belief in God's sovereignty (and her own assuredness in her own salvation) relieves some of the pressure of perfectionism that she feels.

Noelle feels strongly that one of her main purposes in life is to show forth God's love, in whatever setting she happens to be in—and for now, that just happens to be teaching. She has no strong sense of "calling" related to her teaching—"I mean, right now I'm teaching middle school, but I might not do this forever. That's okay." Whatever Noelle does, now and in the future, she believes her responsibility is to do the best she can to the best of her ability and to show forth God's love. She describes God's love as "all-encompassing," "patient," "kind," but she also believes that God's love is "just." She believes God has expectations of those who love him, and her own conception of what it means to love others is informed by her sense of God's love for her. When you love God, showing his love to others is a responsibility, but it's not a chore. Noelle says, "I mean, that's something I innately want to show to people . . . but sure, sometimes I have to remind myself." Showing forth God's love to others is the kind of evangelizing that Noelle is most comfortable with. If she is being kind, patient, and just with the people around her, she may not feel the need to explicitly tell them *why* she is behaving that way until they ask her.

Aside from the much-disparaged bunny, a major feature of Noelle's classroom is the giant chalkboard painted on the back wall. When I first visit, it reads in giant, swoopy, chalky letters, "Be somebody who makes everybody feel like a somebody." By my final visit, the space around the inspirational quote has been filled with chalky handprints, giant kid-drawn flowers, jokes, and the kind of inane mix of braggadocio ("Tyler's the best!" signed by Tyler himself) and fawning (Ms. Andrews, I love you!) that happens when middle schoolers have space, time, and permission to write on a board. When I tell her how much I like her chalkboard wall, Noelle smiles conspiratorially. "The administration didn't want me to do the whole wall. They said I could paint *some* of the back wall, but not the whole thing." I look more carefully—although it looks like the whole back wall is a chalkboard, there's a 1-foot border on each side of the wall that has not been painted in chalkboard paint. "I didn't do the whole thing!" she assures me with a laugh.

Noelle teaches in a middle school that is set in the heart of a hipster-y, newly gentrified downtown area. It's a small town, population-wise, but it makes up part of a larger sprawling metropolitan area, so it feels anything but rural. There's an artisanal tequila store a few steps away from the school, a bakery just behind the school that sells donuts—vegan *and* gluten-free, if you're so inclined—and multiple industrial-chic restaurants with outdoor-eating porches, exposed brick, and neatly painted ductwork. All of it, including the nearly-new middle school that sits just off the main street, gives off the air of modern prosperity—an air that one imagines was carefully orchestrated by savvy city planners. The middle school itself is public, but Noelle says that it "might as well be a magnet school, for all intents and purposes" because it prides itself on a specialized STEAM (science, technology, engineering, arts, and mathematics)–based curriculum and because it allows "permissive transfers" to students who wish to attend the school from outside the zoning area so long as they provide their own transportation to and from the school. The school is only in its third year, and the building itself seems new—from the wide white hallways that feel modern to the built-in security measures—an entrance that you have to buzz into to gain access to the receptionist's office.

Ms. Andrews's room, too, feels shiny and new. There are no traditional school desks, with chairs and writing surfaces soldered together in a utilitarian tangle of metal legs and flat wood. Instead, multiple half-circle and diamond-shaped laminate-topped tables with wheels are pushed together to form circles or long rectangles, surrounded by wheeled chairs. Instead of a traditional classroom with desks in rows, this classroom feels like an open work space at a trendy tech start-up. The feeling is amplified by the fact that after school lets out, Noelle likes to crank up sunny pop music while she works (and while the bunny hops around).

Noelle's classroom reflects a strong sense of order and organization—with bulletin boards full of neatly laminated, symmetrically hung inspirational quotes from various authors paired with classroom expectations (see Figure 4.1). William Shakespeare's quote, typed next to his portrait, for example, is "Better three hours too soon than one minute too late." In bolder, bigger font, the paper declares: "Arrive on time." A smiling picture of Maya Angelou exhorts the class to be kind and respectful; Nelson Mandela urges persistence and determination.

Figure 4.1.

But off the carefully curated bulletin boards are other quotes, too. Silly quotes from some of the students in her class—still-backed onto colored paper and laminated—highlight Noelle's more playful side: "You smurfed this paper!" "Now I know how James Bond feels!" "What would I do without Ms. Andrews' handwriting?" A hand-drawn poster (see Figure 4.2) tacked to the wall lays forth the conditions under which it is okay to blurt out in class: if someone is hurt or ill, if you are on fire, if the room is flooding, if you brought Ms. Andrews Starbucks, if Justin Timberlake has entered the classroom, or if aliens are invading. The poster, of course, is laminated.

Figure 4.2.

Noelle's sense of herself as a teacher is still developing. When she entered teacher training, she imagined herself as a high school teacher because she loves literature. Now, however, she finds that she connects most with kids who are a "little more elementary" in their mindset. Some of this is because she is still trying to figure out classroom management:

> From what I've seen the kids who are more mature also are more sassy . . . and I'm just not good at dealing with that. I'm not the most sarcastic person. So, I don't know. I just like the ones that are still babies.

If Noelle appreciates kids who are still sweet and eager to please, it might also be because she never had an "angsty teenaged phase" herself. She connects most easily with kids who appreciate and enjoy her personality—a self-described silly person who likes to drink tea and talk about her plants.

Noelle struggles to connect with students who have a hard time being good classroom citizens—kids who create "social drama" or who disrupt classroom flow. She is quick to point out that these kids have been failed by the school system, pushed through multiple years of schooling without ever receiving the help they need to succeed—but knowing that doesn't make it any easier to deal with the issues of classroom management that arise (and that Noelle feels fairly unprepared to deal with).

Noelle has a clear idea of how she wants to perform being a "good teacher," but she doesn't always feel like she lives up to her own expectations. She defines a good teacher this way:

> It's somebody who can connect with their kids on a social level and emotional level, but can also teach them the content they're supposed to be teaching in a way that helps kids master it wherever they are—at all levels.

For Noelle, the social and emotional connections of a classroom are just as important—if not more important—than academic achievement and content mastery. She is fine with not every kid getting an "A" or mastering every standard, as long as they "give their best" and are "aware of the social cues and factors going on around them. ". . . Honestly, that's the biggest thing," she says as she gathers her hair in a ponytail and then drops it again. "Most people aren't thoughtful and I expect people to be thoughtful." Interpersonal relationships, kindness, and being in community as a class matter to Noelle—and she expects herself to be the primary example of those qualities.

Teaching has been harder than Noelle expected. She finds herself constantly anxious about time management—an area that had always been easy for her in her student life. If something is going to drive her out of the profession, it will be this niggling anxiety about having forgotten to do one of the dozens of small tasks that make up a teacher's administrative responsibility. Classroom management, too, is a challenge she hasn't yet mastered. Although she believes in giving grace to her students, she also has a very particular view of how students should show respect to a teacher. She points out several times that she doesn't mind being "the mean teacher" because her students need to learn to be responsible. There's a frustration there, however: If kids didn't act out, if they stayed on task, if they controlled their words and their actions, she wouldn't have to be "the mean teacher" who gives out silent lunches and has to "speak very sternly to them and scare them a little bit." In Noelle's ideal world, she would be able to perform the identity of the perennially sunny, cheerful, and kind teacher because her students' behavior wouldn't necessitate "calling them out" or getting "personally annoyed" at them. Because Noelle was such a compliant student, she readily admits that she doesn't always understand why students act out or have difficulty doing what they are supposed to do.

Moments of Hesitation—Showing God's Love

One of Noelle's moments of hesitation as a religious teacher centers firmly in her struggle to show God's love to her students. There are two real points of hesitation here: First, how does she make sure that her personality, her performance of teacher, and her general worldview accurately exemplify the joy that comes from feeling God's grace? The second is perhaps more directly tied to pedagogical practice: How does she find the balance between showing forth the love of Jesus by giving grace even when kids don't deserve it with the responsibility of also showing forth the love of God by holding kids to high standards of conduct?

Performing Joy

During my last interview with Noelle, she says, "I have something for you!" She pulls out a leopard-print fanny pack and says, "Now we can be twins!" She gestures to the sunflower-print fanny pack on her desk. She purchased herself the fanny pack after she realized she needed something to carry all her *teaching stuff* around with her as she conferences with kids. "I've mostly packed it for you," she said. "But you'll have to add some stuff to it." I immediately tighten the straps of the fanny pack around my hips and give Noelle a hug to thank her. I'm delighted by the gift, but mostly I'm amazed at the ingenuity and problem-solving those fanny packs represent. A peek inside Noelle's fanny pack, which she straps on while she's teaching and moving around the classroom, reveals it is stuffed with unexpectedly helpful teaching supplies for every situation: a red pen for marking papers, an Expo marker to write on the tops of the laminated tables or on the whiteboards, hand sanitizer ("Because, middle schoolers."), lip balm, a Sharpie marker, star stickers to reward really excellent work, her room keys, a whistle for the playground, Wite-Out in case kids get anxious about writing the wrong thing, breath mints ("Sometimes the kids come to school with dragon breath!"), a hair clip so that she can keep her hair out of the way, and a protein bar in case she (or a student) needs a little pick-me-up. She has since purchased a fanny pack in various prints for all the teachers on her instructional team. This kind of organization, preparedness, thoughtfulness, and generosity is typical of Noelle, and these qualities are an integral part of her identity as a religious teacher.

As a religious teacher, Noelle doesn't feel a specific call to be a teacher and has tried to purposely not view herself as a Christian savior to the kids in her classroom:

> We just can't save all the children . . . and be like a counselor to them all. I've tried not to put that on myself but I see that very much being how you view yourself if you are a Christian and a teacher.

Noelle expresses discomfort with "these two images aligning"—the overlap between her conception of what a good teacher does and what a good Christian does is something she tries to push against. That being said, Noelle would find it hard to separate her identity as a Christian from any career that she follows because she does believe that her purpose in life "is to glorify God and further the spread of the Gospel and that doesn't matter what career I'm in." Although Noelle states that she is being "very intentional in identifying" that evangelical attitude in herself, she has come to a place of peace about what that evangelizing might look like for her in her teaching career.

Noelle believes that part of her call as an evangelical Christian is to evangelize no matter what career she is in, but for her, that evangelism most often looks like a performance of happiness, joy, peace, and kindness with the understanding that others will see that and want that joy for themselves. Once they approach her with questions about why she is so happy, so joyful, so peaceful, and so kind, then she feels like she can honestly have conversations about her religious beliefs and the ways in which those beliefs have shaped who she is. This is true in her life outside of school, but she is especially aware of constructing her teaching identity around these principles. She is aware that there are limits on how and when she should ethically talk explicitly about her faith with kids, and so she purposefully has created a teacher identity that exemplifies the qualities that she thinks set Christians apart.

In our final focus group, Noelle shares with Mei Lin and Mallory an instance in which her indirect evangelism paid off and she felt validated in her approach. Noelle uses the Remind app to send kids and parents reminders about upcoming assignments, tests, and so on. One student—"this tiny little girl"—kept sending her Bible verses through the app. The girl then messaged: "Ms. Andrews, I have a question. Are you a Christian or do you just go to church?" When Mallory asks Noelle how she responded, Noelle shrugs and says, "I was like, 'Yeah, I am. Have a good evening!'" The important part of this story for Noelle, however, is the student's response: "She messaged back and was like, 'I KNEW IT. I AM TOO!' in all caps because she's 11. 'THAT'S WHY YOU'RE SO HAPPY ALL THE TIME!'" I point out how interesting it is that Noelle's happiness is what the girl points out as the distinguishing Christian characteristic, particularly because Noelle has talked about the pressure she feels to perform happiness. Noelle smiles and admits, "I felt like I was making a difference . . . it was kind of validating."

Although she is very comfortable with evangelism through example, Noelle's carefully maintained cheerful-and-joyful-in-Christ teaching identity was challenged when her boyfriend of many years broke up with her right before the Christmas break. In our very first interview, we are talking about her first year of teaching when a neighboring teacher pops her head in and asks, "Are you okay?" After the brief exchange, Noelle turns to me and says with quivering lips, "They all want to check on me because my boyfriend broke up with me this week." On the recording of our conversation, I fumble with the recorder and say, "Here, I'm going to turn this off for a minute," and then the recording clicks back on and we carry on, both of our voices determinedly bright and too cheerful for the heartbreaking conversation that was carried on in the 20 minutes that the brief break in the recording represents.

In subsequent interviews and Flipgrid posts, she wonders how she will manage being honest with her students about her heartbreak while also trying to show forth the cheerful goodness of a Christian faith. Perhaps unspoken is the worry that if she fails to maintain the cheery exterior for her students, she is failing in being an example of God's love for her students. "So my ultimate sense of joy is in Christ," she says, "but . . . a lot of that gets wrapped up in other things and relationships and part of that really keeps me in check, like, 'Hey, what am I really focusing on?" She blows her bangs back from her face in a quick huff. "But on the other hand, that doesn't mean the things that go on in my life don't matter. Because they do. Like, a lot." Here Noelle is thinking about what emotions she is allowed to have if her joy is really in Christ. "I feel a responsibility to really model that for my students," she says.

School becomes a place where Noelle feels she has to balance her very real, very sad, very hard emotions in the present with her equally real and joyful feelings about her faith. Noelle admits that in this moment of wanting to present both honestly *and* happily at a time when the two emotions don't seem to fit together, she often just chooses to fake cheerfulness, sometimes for her own benefit and sometimes for the kids' benefit. For herself, she says, "I mean, a nice thing about school is you can just kind of pretend to be somebody else until the kids go home at the end of the day, and I think that helped me do better myself, too." For the kids, she performs fake cheerfulness because she wants to model grace under difficult situations:

> It really frustrates me when my students feel something and get frustrated and it overwhelms every single aspect of their life for the rest of the day. So in some ways, I'm showing them how to just keep going when stuff is hard.

The drawback to this approach, Noelle points out, is that she makes the struggle sound easier than it actually is. She sees value, too, in modeling for kids that "sometimes you can't just put a smile on it and make it all okay." However, at the end of the day, she doesn't have time to have the complicated conversations about emotions and honesty and perseverance because she has two sets of standards[3] she has to cover and not enough time to get that done. "I already get distracted enough as it is talking about my dog to them," she says with a half-smile. As with many of her moments of hesitation, Noelle feels like she has made choices that she is satisfied with. "I kind of thought I did serve everyone," she muses because pretending to be cheerful models an important lesson to students while also giving her an opportunity to try to move past her sadness, a move that she can't see herself making if she just spends all day "being sad and meditating on that."

Giving Grace

The second dilemma that Noelle faces around showing forth God's love through her classroom practice is figuring out how to model God's love for kids through her own navigation of a position of power—a position where she can choose to show mercy or insist on perfection. Noelle's religious conceptions of repentance, obedience, and grace play a large part in the hesitations that she has around managing kids and assigning grades in a public school learning environment. In our first focus group, she shares her frustrations with the current standards-based assessment movement:

> Overall, I see the school system and administration showing [the kids] more grace than I would in a lot of ways. Like with grades for example, I can't give a child a zero or a[n] NTI [not turned in] and . . . that child will pass my class because they've turned in one assignment all year long. So, do I show them grace . . . or do I follow what they actually did—which was nothing—and fail them? . . . My faith and my worldview says that I should show you grace and mercy, but at the same time, I feel like that comes up against the same [religiously informed] mindset of justice and accountability.

Noelle's faith and religiously informed worldview cause her to always consider the exact balance of grace and justice that will "bring this child to learning" and the imprecision of that formula is frustrating. Even more frustrating is when she feels that she understands the balance required for this particular kid or this particular moment of classroom management and the school administration stands in the way of her being able to perform it.

While grading and assessment are frustrating for Noelle, the day-to-day management of dozens of children's emotions, behavior, and classroom engagement is where Noelle spends the most time considering what grace looks like in a classroom setting. If assessment is an area that Noelle tends to approach with a justice and fairness mindset, then interpersonal relationships are where Noelle wants most to be graceful, forgiving, and kind. This grace, however, often seems to be loosely (and perhaps even unconsciously) tied to the religious concept of repentance. From a religious standpoint, Noelle believes that when she does something wrong—which to her means that she does something against the laws of God as set forth in the Bible—that she asks for forgiveness by praying for repentance and doing her best to make amends for any wrong she has caused to others. Noelle repents to receive forgiveness, and God continuously forgives those who repent. Noelle may unconsciously follow this pattern in her classroom management strategies even as she explicitly states that her goal is to show grace to kids *even when they don't deserve it*:

> [The administration won't let us] grade homework, so if a kid doesn't turn in their homework I give them silent lunch. Sorry, there's no exception, you have to sit in silent lunch. This week I had two kids who didn't bring their reading log homework with them. They sat there—like, one of them never does his homework anyway, I think he's done his homework twice the whole year, but the other girl, she was probably about to burst into tears, and so I went over to them and . . . I said, "If you do your homework over the weekend and bring it to me Monday before lunch, you don't have to sit in silent lunch today. But if you don't bring it to me then, you've got silent lunch on Monday."

What Noelle classifies as grace here (letting the kids miss the silent lunch today if they bring their homework later) might be more accurately considered as grace after first recognizing penitence from a student. So while she says there's "no exception" to the rule, when she sees a student who is "about to burst into tears" and is visibly performing remorse or anxiety over missing the assignment, *then* she moves to a stance of forgiveness and grace (or at least a stay of justice). It seems likely from the way she discusses the other student who forgot his homework that she would not have extended grace to him in this instance if the other girl had not also been included because he "never does his homework anyway." Noelle also offers the students a way to make amends and make the wrong right (bringing the forgotten homework on Monday before lunch)—an important piece of her beliefs around repentance, forgiveness, and grace.

Moments of Hesitation—Gender, Sexuality, and Saying the Right Thing

Noelle skims through most of her moments of hesitation with a sense of satisfaction in the way that she balances the needs of her students, the legal requirements of her job, and her personal faith. Because she sees so much of her job as loving kids and exemplifying mature behavior and because her conception of God's sovereignty minimizes her own sense of power, Noelle feels fairly comfortable in the choices she's made about how honest to be about her own heartbreak, for example, or how she struggles with what love and care might look like in classroom management. If there is an area where Noelle seems to truly experience a moment of hesitation—an aporia that she can't quite bridge the impossibility of—it is in issues of gender and sexuality. Her interaction with Hannah, her favorite student, a seventh grader who is transitioning from female to male, is particularly sticky for Noelle—both situationally and in her memory.

"Transitioning"—A Portrait in Poetry

I don't know what my reaction is supposed to be

Her mom said to me,
"Ignore her fashion choices.
Hannah is a girl."
But then
I started hearing kids
talking
Like saying,
No, Hannah goes by 'he' now.
She wants to be called he."
Just amongst themselves.

I have a good relationship with her

I mean,
none of them know
who they are

Every morning she comes in my class

The media does influence that
It is very much projected on them

I make her a cup of tea.
We have a tea party.
We show each other pictures of our dogs.

I mean, the LGBT community and
being like that
Is very much in the popular media

She didn't come out as gay or lesbian
She just told me that she sees herself
as a boy
and wants to be called he

I don't think you can change your sexual orientation and have God be okay with that, but

I don't know how I could say that in a way
That wouldn't shut them down.

The way most Christians talk about it is very
off-putting.
It's off-putting to me.

I feel personal guilt
I feel uncomfortable
I feel conflicted

It's off-putting to them.
That's not going to make them want to follow Jesus.

But I had thought about what I
was going to say:

"It doesn't matter what you want to be
called; it doesn't change
who you are."

Gender Trouble

This experience with Hannah comes up over and over and over in our conversations in ways that other experiences with kids don't. Noelle seems to be regrappling with the emotion of the situation every time we talk about it; sometimes she seems to be looking for approval that she made the right choice in what she said; other times, she seems to be laying out a case for why her response was the most appropriate possible response. But the deep discomfort she feels around issues of gender and sexuality are always evident—from the way she continues to refer to Hannah as a "she," although Hannah has asked to be addressed as "he," to the way that she twists her mouth as she tells or retells the story. It's clear that Noelle cares deeply about Hannah and that Hannah adores Noelle, but equally clear is that Noelle doesn't know how she can manage her Christian responsibility to love Hannah with what she views as the equally Christian responsibility to stand up for Christian values around gender and sexuality.

Noelle shares another incident involving Hannah that makes plain her deep affection and sympathy for Hannah. As part of the project-based curriculum, Hannah was paired with another student with whom she had "a difficult relationship," a student whom Noelle characterizes as "very intense" and "on edge." One of the teachers on the teaching team found a note from Hannah to her project partner on the floor one day. Noelle paraphrases Hannah's note:

> I'm really sorry about the way I treat you. I have to just ignore you when we're working together . . . it's my coping mechanism because if I don't ignore you . . . I'm going to get really angry and I'm going to blow up and say some things I will regret and I will probably make you cry. I'm dealing with a lot of things right now and I'm getting help for them—with them, but I'm doing my best. I'm really sorry I offended you. . . . By the way, I prefer to go by "he" and "him." If you want to call me "she" that's fine, but don't call me "that weird it person thing" because that really offends me.

Noelle is moved by this note—by the maturity of it, by the sadness that her favorite student is being called "weird it person thing," by the overall tone of reconciliation and accountability. Noelle tells me over and over that Hannah is her favorite student. But she is clearly also deeply troubled by

Hannah's transition. I point out as kindly as I can that this is an interesting moment for Noelle because she cares so deeply for Hannah and she doesn't want to ever treat anyone hatefully, which she perceives other Christians doing to those who identify as transgender, and yet, throughout our entire conversation, she never once refers to Hannah as "he" or "him" even when Hannah has asked her to use those pronouns.

"No. Yeah," she says, acknowledging a hit. "I'm really—I don't know. I'm very conflicted. I don't know what to do with that either." In classroom situations, she simply avoids using pronouns to refer to Hannah, choosing instead to always use his name.

I ask her why she is hesitant to use Hannah's preferred pronouns. She talks about how Hannah is too young—only 13 years old—to already know who she is, and she has a hesitancy to affirm an identity that she sees as a possibly temporary confusion or teenage whim. Noelle speaks quickly, her words tumbling one after the other, as she explains:

> [Hannah's] world is so infiltrated by what is going on in the common culture right now. "Be whoever you want to be. Be gay. Be lesbian. Be bisexual. Be transgender." . . . Access to the internet just makes things even more confusing for them. Maybe you do really genuinely feel like you are a boy, but I don't think at 13 years old, you really know who you are.

Noelle's religiously informed beliefs around gender and sexuality—that people are made in the image of God and they can't change their sexual orientation or gender and expect God to be okay with that[4]—causes her to frame what she can only view as Hannah's gender troubles from a skeptical viewpoint. This skepticism means that instead of engaging supportively with Hannah's transition, Noelle largely chooses to skirt the issue, to engage in verbal wordplay that allows her to *seem* supportive while still drawing a clear distinction in her own mind between what it means to support Hannah while not supporting Hannah's transition.

As we unpack the moment of hesitation that Noelle feels around Hannah's transition, I ask her to work through the aporia she feels she is navigating. To whom and to what does she feel responsible? She says matter-of-factly,

> Well, I'm responsible for making sure that my student feels loved and accepted. And I'm responsible to myself and my faith in God, and the fact

> that I believe that God created you in his image the way that you are and that's who you are supposed to be even if you might feel tensions to identify as somebody else. That's not who God made you to be.

In short, what Noelle feels pulled between is her very religiously informed conception of what it means to love students and to show forth God's love to her students and her equally religiously informed conception of gender and sexuality. This is a circle that Noelle can't ever quite square, and so she ends up trying to walk the line between these two demands—"I really like to walk the line," she says with a shrug. She's not quite Solomon with the baby,[5] insisting on a final and irrevocable declaration one way or the other; instead, she's Peter receiving revelation about keeping kosher post-Messiah,[6] looking for a medium ground that hurts no one and compromises nothing.

What this aporia opens up for Noelle is a linguistic wordplay of her own: "I told her, 'It doesn't matter what you want to be called. You're still the same person no matter what your name is. . . . Like, I was very careful with how I said that because I'm still . . ." She trails off here, her own uncertainty evident. The care with which she crafted this statement is evident, too: Hannah can pick up this statement as an expression of support, acceptance, and love, which is how Noelle wants her to pick it up. But this statement also allows Noelle to be true to her core belief that you're still the same person God made you to be no matter what pronouns you use or what name you use. It's a message that has a purposeful double meaning: acceptance and love if read one way and uncompromising belief in God-ordained gender and sexuality if read the other way.

What might be most important here is that Noelle intentionally means for her statement to be able to be read in both ways. She feels the call to love and accept students at the exact moments when she also feels the call to uphold what she sees as God's laws around gender and sexuality. With this dual call, she thinks deeply about what she might say that answers both seemingly opposed calls.

Looking Forward

At the end of her first year of teaching, with that pesky rabbit farmed out to a student for the summer, Noelle reviewed her first year of teaching. Although she tended to be hard on herself during the year—particularly about classroom management—in hindsight, she thinks maybe she didn't give herself enough credit because she really did form meaningful and important relationships with so many of her students. She's getting ready for her second year of teaching in the same school with the same teaching assignment. She's looking forward to knowing so much more about what she's doing than she did on her first day of her first year of teaching. On a personal note, she assures me that she's genuinely doing okay now regarding her breakup. The breakup might just have been a blessing—she's moving in with friends and making life decisions based on what *she* wants in the future, not just on what might happen in her relationship. With her sunny, cheerful disposition more firmly in place, she remains committed to showing forth God's love in her classroom by being joyful, patient, and happy.

Discussion

Noelle's performance of teacher is deeply informed and made possible by her Christian discourse. Without her Christian identity, Noelle herself wonders if she would want to be a teacher since she sees her work in the classroom as so closely aligning with the work of a Christian. The particular doctrines and discursive figurations that make Noelle's pedagogical stances and practices possible center around her understanding of herself as a person who is called to do God's work in all aspects of her life, including her teaching life. Perhaps the most salient takeaways of how Noelle's religious identity makes her teacher identity possible might be enumerated as follows:

1. Because Noelle sees teaching as a fundamentally Christian act, she works to perform a version of teacherness that centers joy, patience, and happiness—traits that she views as being the fruits of living a Christlike life. In theory, if she is joyful, patient, and happy enough, her students will be drawn to a relationship with Jesus because of her example. Being a Christian teacher puts an extra layer of pressure on Noelle to perform kindness in a way that mimics or personifies Christian love.

2. Noelle's teacher practice, particularly in terms of her interactions with students, is made possible by her Christian-based concepts of repentance, forgiveness, grace, sovereignty, and perfection.

3. Noelle feels a great deal of hesitation around issues of gender and sexuality in the classroom. She wants to show how Christians might show unconditional love to those who identify as LGBTQ+, but she also wants to be true to her own belief that God cannot ever be okay with those identities.

Welcoming in the other, as Derrida would phrase it then, is an important part of Noelle's stance toward the students in her classroom. She *wants* to see them, speak to them (especially if it's about her plants or her puppy), address them, and welcome them—particularly if doing so can be read as the fruits of a Christian belief and life. But this might be hospitality based on a desire to evangelize, or to welcome the other with the intent of making them not-other. Classroom discipline for Noelle mimics Christian repentance and may create spaces for connection with (and unconditional welcoming of) the other only if the other can perform the version of Christian repentance and godly sorrow that Noelle recognizes.

Where Noelle's performance of Christian teacher becomes uncomfortably challenging is the focus of this study, and for Noelle, these moments of hesitation and uncertainty are often tied to sexuality and gender. Noelle, who wants to be obedient to God's command to stand up for absolute truth and who also wants to care for a student who is struggling to transition in an environment that is not always very understanding, employs linguistic ambiguity and double meanings to try to achieve both of her goals at the same time. I don't read Noelle in this situation as necessarily exercising the right of the host to set limits on hospitality, to determine who is considered worthy of hospitality and who can be relegated to a state of "not-being." This is not an examination of a moment of arrival with regard to Hannah. What Noelle's experience with Hannah's gender transition might be best viewed as is an examination of how hospitality changes and responds when the conditionally/unconditionally welcomed other asks difficult questions, "shakes up the threatening dogmatism of the paternal *logos*" (Derrida, 1997/2000, p. 5), and challenges the comfortable assumptions of the host. Certainly for Noelle, who admits to not having much interaction with the LGBTQ+ community, her affection for Hannah amid her transition opens up discomfort or a space of interior alterity, a space that she freely admits she "doesn't know quite what to do with."

If Noelle's grappling with Hannah's transition is a moment of arrival, perhaps it's a moment of arrival for Noelle herself—a moment in which she has to face the otherness within herself, account for the sociopolitical responsibilities of her own religious identity and beliefs and weigh what violences she is and isn't willing to enact on her "favorite student." Furthermore, I see Noelle working to consider how language itself might be a violent form of hospitality. We might consider here Derrida's (1997/2000) urge that perhaps unconditional hospitality consists of "suspending language, a particular determinate language . . . which herald[s] so many required conditions" (p. 135). While Noelle can't quite suspend language or the conditions of her hospitality, she *is* making moves to reconcile her own ways of being and knowing with welcoming the other through linguistic play. Noelle's unease with using Hannah's preferred pronouns might be balanced by the care with which she crafts a statement of response to Hannah's transition that can be read as supportive as she tries to welcome in Hannah—and the otherness of Hannah that she cannot, as an evangelical Christian, unconditionally welcome—without giving up her place as host of the classroom.

Notes

1. This means, at the simplest level, that God has selected them to be saved or has determined their salvation *for* them.
2. When Noelle refers to herself as "reformed," she is generally referencing her Calvinist-informed beliefs. These beliefs are sometimes called the Five Points of Calvinism and are often taught as part of an acronym, TULIP: T—Total Depravity, U—Unconditional Election, L—Limited Atonement, I—Irresistible Grace, and P—Perseverance of the Saint. In layperson's terms, this means that "man [is in] need of salvation (Total depravity) and . . . God takes steps to save his people. He elects (Unconditional election), then he sends Jesus to atone for the sins of the elect (Limited atonement), then he irresistibly draws his people to faith (Irresistible grace) and finally works to cause them to persevere to the end (Perseverance of the saints)" (Piper, 1985, "At the Heart of Biblical Theology"). It is important to clarify that not all evangelicals consider themselves to be reformed. Noelle's beliefs about unconditional election and limited atonement often set her apart in evangelical circles.
3. Because Noelle teaches a humanities course, she is responsible for covering both the social studies curriculum standards and the language arts curriculum standards. Her students are evaluated on both sets of standards in their county's end-of-course exams.
4. It is worth pointing out here that Noelle's beliefs cause her to view hetero- and cis-identities as the norm. It is why she can't fathom Hannah making a decision at 13 to switch to male pronouns, positioning him as confused and too young to know his own gender and sexuality while simultaneously believing that the hetero- and cis-identities within her classroom know their own minds and are not confused about their gender and sexuality at all.
5. A reference to the judgment of Solomon, a Bible story in which the Hebrew king, Solomon, rules between two women who both claim to be the mother of a child. Solomon rules that

the baby should be cut in half and that half of it be given to each woman to keep. Upon hearing the judgment, one woman asks for the baby to be given to the other woman so that the baby can live, while the other woman agrees it is a fair ruling. Solomon determines the relationships and feelings of the women by their response to his judgment and gives the baby to the woman who asked for the baby's life to be spared.

6. In the New Testament, Peter has a vision where he considers whether it is necessary for those who follow Christ to keep kosher dietary laws. Instead of directly addressing dietary regulations, his takeaway from the vision is that God showed him that he should not call any man unclean, a neat linguistic workaround that makes space within the nascent Christian Church for both keeping and abandoning kosher dietary practices. Another example might be Paul to the Corinthians on the matter of eating in social settings food that may have been sacrificed to idols (other gods). His advice opens multiple interpretations, but the most common reading of the chapter is that it cannot harm a Christian to eat food sacrificed to gods that do not exist and that it is not worth alienating those who do not know or fully understand God's laws on a small point of doctrine.

References

Derrida, J. (2000) *Of hospitality: Anne Dufourmantelle invites Jacques Derrida to respond* (R. Bowlby, Trans.). Stanford University Press. (Original work published 1997)

Piper, J. (1985). *What we believe about the five points of Calvinism.* https://www.desiringgod.org/articles/what-we-believe-about-the-five-points-of-calvinism

CHAPTER FIVE

Portraits of Mei: Evangelism Everywhere

The first time I visit Mei Lin's classroom, I compliment her on her stylish ankle boots—yellow suede with a chunky heel. "Oh, thanks," she says, "I got these a long time ago, and every time I think about throwing them away I get another compliment on them." She stretches out one ankle so I can look at the boot more carefully. She is a young-looking third-year teacher—slender, shortish, pretty. She manages to distinguish herself from the kids only by wearing cardigans and thick-framed glasses. As she walks me into her classroom, there's a student there working on makeup work, and all around the classroom are poster charts that her classes have been working on examining the ethos, pathos, and logos within the political arguments of the popular Broadway musical *Hamilton!* (Miranda, 2016).

Because she teaches English-language learners (ELLs), there are sentence stems on the board to support her students' language and writing processes as they analyze the rhetorical moves of the Broadway versions of Hamilton and Jefferson (see Figure 5.1). "I've really hit my stride with planning this year," she comments as I walk around and look at her students' work. "I finally understand how to tie everything together throughout the whole year and how to scaffold really well."

Mei teaches in a large high school—so large that as I pull up after school, I have to wait to pull into the parking lot for what seems an eternity as yellow school bus after yellow school bus after yellow school bus lurches away from the building. The school itself is built in the same style as nearly every other high school in the district, with a large central area at the entrance that functions as the cafeteria during the school day, although the student body has to eat in three different shifts. As I walk in, it's currently being utilized by the cheer squad, and they're stretching, toe touching, and chattering.

This isn't an inner-city school by any means, but the effects of gentrification have pushed many of the former residents of the sprawling metropolis to nearby suburbs like this one—a short 30-minute drive from the city center with slightly more affordable housing as well. Ethnic supermarkets abound in the surrounding area, and what's most notable is just how many different ethnicities are represented. There's a Mexican *panetería* next to a Korean market next to a Thai market next to a Jamaican restaurant that advertises its authentic jerk-flavored meat. There are churches with small cemeteries surrounding them right next to the school, and the church board announces next week's services in English. But a short 3-minute drive down the road, other church boards announce their own services in Spanish, Korean, or Ukrainian. Area church titles reflect the strong presence of immigrant populations: Vietnamese Church of Christ, Korean Methodist, and Ghanaian Christian Ministry are just a few of the churches that cater to worshippers who come from a variety of linguistic and ethnic heritages.

Like most ELL teachers, Mei uses English as the lingua franca of her classroom for practical and educational reasons. Her students speak a variety of languages, but her job is to teach them American literature while also building their English-language skills. Once students reach a certain level of

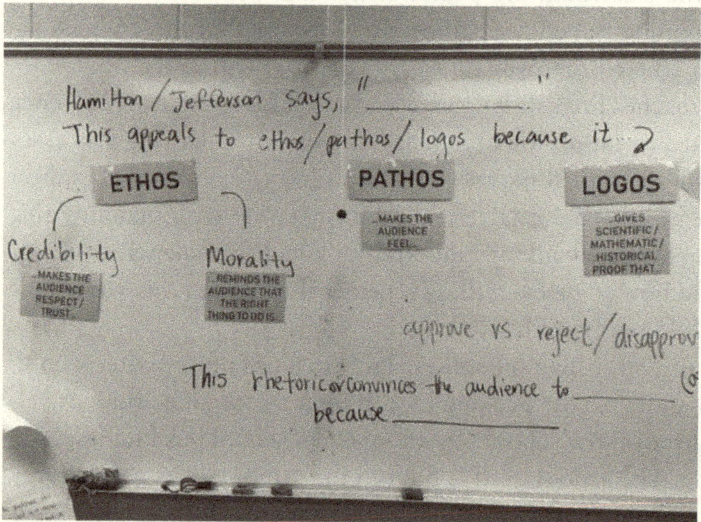

Figure 5.1.

language proficiency, they no longer qualify for the sheltered services that Mei provides within her classroom, and they are moved to regular education classes. Although many of Mei's students are still developing language proficiency, Mei's class uses the same standards and basic curricular structure as other American literature classes. Mei's confidence in her ability to accomplish all the things she has to do has grown since her first year of teaching when, she confesses, she really felt like she "was just surviving."

One of the things Mei is most proud of is the way that she's thinking about learning as a linear process that builds on itself in increasingly complex tasks (see Figure 5.2). One of the things she is trying to teach her students how to do is to monitor their own learning and understand what they can do when they aren't "getting it."

For the rhetoric unit she is teaching when I visit her, she's broken that linear process down in this way: First, students have to be able to define rhetorical devices; second, they have to be able to identify rhetorical devices in the texts they study; third, students have to be able to analyze the ways in which rhetorical devices impact an argument and the way an argument is framed; fourth, students have to be able to evaluate the effectiveness of an author's use of rhetorical devices; and, fifth, students have to be able to argue their own issues and beliefs using rhetorical devices.[1]

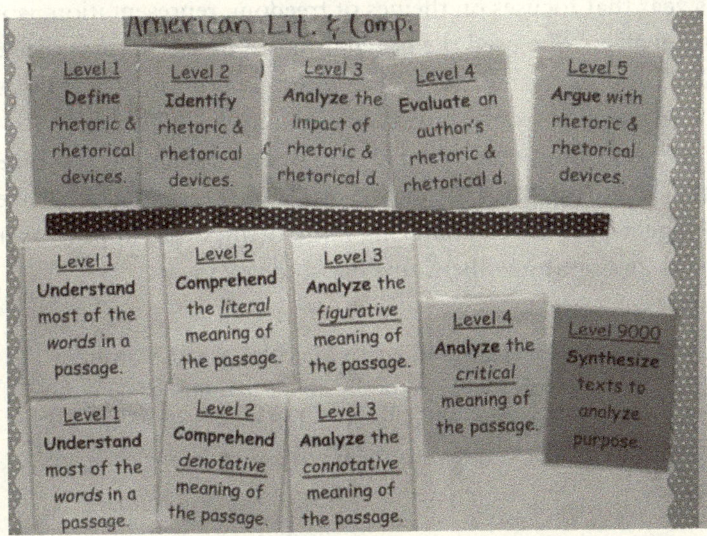

Figure 5.2.

As Mei works her students through this linear process, if she notices a student struggling to complete one of the tasks, she believes that the student probably cannot complete the current task because they have not fully mastered the level of thinking that comes before it. Her solution is to create remediation that attends to the previous level's tasks.

Her students have picked up the concept of leveling skills as well to talk about their own learning. "We were doing all Level 3 one day and one of the girls was like, 'Miss, I don't think any of us understand this; can we just do a lesson on Level 2? I don't even think I understand Level 2!'" For Mei, the shared language of learning as a leveled process gives her a sense that she understands where every student is in the learning process and a sense that she knows where they need to go next to master a standard. She says, "I was completely unprepared [to teach a Level 2 lesson,] but I was like, here let me throw something at you because you requested it and you're right." Most important, Mei is proud that her students have begun to monitor where their own learning process is breaking down regarding the leveled steps she has provided for them.

When I ask Mei what she values in a curriculum, she says without hesitation, "Efficiency and authenticity. Relevance and engagement, real-world impact—I think I need to hit all of those things for a unit to be worth teaching." What this has meant in practical terms is that Mei has created a curriculum this year that focuses on themes of freedom, representation, isolationism, and globalism. She used the popular movie *Black Panther* (Feige & Coogler, 2018) and partnered the movie with texts on the Black Lives Matter movement, speeches from Martin Luther King, Jr.; Malcolm X; Patrick Henry; and others. Additionally, her classes watched multiple YouTube videos that critiqued and analyzed the movie. For Mei, every assignment she gives feeds the bigger purpose of analyzing large themes that appear over and over in American literature. She wants her students to

> think about what Patrick Henry would say to Malcolm X and Martin Luther King, Jr. because Patrick Henry is totally about fighting for equality and fighting for freedom. But then Malcolm X and Martin Luther King are fighting against Patrick Henry's descendants. It points out the hypocrisy of White Americans.

She's proud of the way that she's been able to put *Black Panther*, a movie her students really loved, in conversation with rigorous academic texts: "They're like, Oh! Killmonger is like the Malcolm X character because he wants to fight! And T'Challa is like Martin Luther King, Jr., right?" But what she's most proud of is the fact that her units this year are "accomplishing a lot of things at once." So yes, of course she's teaching standards, and she's teaching academic vocabulary (like *ethos*, *pathos*, and *logos*), and she's teaching reading skills and writing skills, but she also feels like she's teaching students to connect all of that learning to a bigger project: critiquing the way that "freedom" in the United States has always been closely tied to race and power.

Mei teaches in a school with a large Hispanic population—almost half the student body—but her ELL students come from all over the world. She has taught or currently teaches students from the Middle East who speak Arabic or Farsi as their first language, students from South and Central America who speak Spanish as their first language, and students from Russia and other former Soviet Union countries who speak Russian as their first language. Part of what drew Mei to teaching language arts to language learners was her own experience as a young child. She moved to the United States at the age of 8, and she remembers well the frustration of learning a new language while also trying to understand a new culture. Mei still holds Chinese citizenship, and when I ask her if she identifies as Chinese American or Chinese, she blinks at me. "I'm Chinese. I don't have my American citizenship, so I guess you should just say I'm Chinese?" She laughs. "I've never even really thought about that." Chinese is her first language and the language still spoken in her home, but Mei worked very hard as a teenager to not become just fluent in English but to master the ins and outs of the language. She discovered that she loved to write. Even with her busy life as a teacher, she continues to make time to write a blog about her life experiences with a wry, sarcastic voice and a bent toward religious introspection.

Mei grew up attending a Chinese church, but when part of the congregation split off to form a separate group made up primarily of second-generation Chinese Americans, Mei and her family chose to join the splinter group. The two groups share the same building and share building projects, but aside from that, they are distinct congregations with their own ways of doing things. Mei Lin volunteers as a Sunday school teacher, attends weekly Bible studies, and is very active within her own congregation.[2]

Although her church is "nondenominational," she feels that "the leadership teaches in a very Calvinist or Reformed way."[3] When I ask her what that means, she says, "In a joking way, it means that we actually take the Bible seriously. We look at the context of the culture of the Bible and think about . . . what the spirit of the law is." The Bible explicitly states, for example, that women shouldn't wear jewelry, but Mei's Bible reading practices lead her to question what the equivalent of jewelry might be in today's society instead of thinking about jewelry itself as forbidden. "The verse," she explains to me,

> focuses a lot on the way that women express where their priorities are and how you should let the spirit or a gentleness adorn you. So, it's more thinking about how you behave and portray yourself as a Christian woman than thinking about not wearing jewelry.

Mei takes the Bible seriously and views it as a book that can help her navigate modern issues if she focuses on the principles being taught or the "spirit of the law."

Mei's religious beliefs are all-encompassing. Because she believes that all creation (the natural world) reveals characteristics of God to humankind, she sees examples of God's goodness all around her:

> I've been taught to look for the characteristics of God everywhere. I mean, like if I see a mote of dust floating in the air, I have to think, oh man, that's basically me. I'm just floating in the air without a sense of control. I don't know where I go. But God is like the wind that will take me to the right place. Literally everywhere—you're supposed to look at God and see God and be reminded that in the moment, you need to worship God.

Mei looks for these signs of God everywhere, but her ultimate authority on God's characteristics is the Bible. Mei's speech is peppered with Bible references and allusions to biblical characters. It's not uncommon for her to explain herself by saying, "So in Romans[4] it says . . ." or "I'm pretty sure Paul[5] said . . ." The Bible is the authority she appeals to on points of doctrine and to frame her conversations.

One phrase that comes up several times as Mei explains her beliefs to me is a phrase that she credits to John Piper, a Reformed Baptist pastor and author of multiple religious books: "We do not flee from sin. We are pursuing holiness." For Mei, this distinction is important. She doesn't want to do the right thing only out of fear of sinning because she trusts that Jesus died for her sins and that her sins are covered. Instead, she wants to obey out of a desire to please God as a reaction to what He has done for her. A huge part of that is taking the opportunity to evangelize whenever possible. Like most evangelical Christians, Mei feels called to share God's love with others. Mei dismisses a softer, less direct form of evangelism (such as being cheerful or making kids feel loved) as being an incomplete reading of the Bible's call to evangelize:

> The way people have [evangelized] in the Bible has always been very explicit. . . . Every single time, like in every story, people are being very explicit with their words—almost rude—when they evangelize. And so, I think if I'm basing [my sense of how to evangelize] on the model of how Jesus and his disciples did it, it would have to be with words.

Evangelism is not only one of Mei's key points of belief, but it's also how she measures the depth of her commitment to God and her own spiritual health. When she has the most faith in God, she has no fear about evangelizing to anyone "whether it's a random stranger and it's a super awkward conversation and you're just like getting it out there and then you're not going to see each other ever again." She pauses for a beat and then adds, "Maybe in heaven, which means it worked." She shrugs as if the outcome of salvation for someone else is less important than her own willingness to evangelize.

During the final focus group meeting, Mei, Noelle, and Mallory discussed the differences in their own beliefs and what those differences make (im)possible for them as teachers. Mei draws a distinction between her own beliefs about God's sovereignty and the other participants that makes this more direct form of evangelism more possible for her. All three teachers use the phrase "God can turn it to good," and "it" can mean anything from their own disobedience to difficult life challenges or situations. Although Noelle and Mallory both use this concept to explain why they feel at peace with not directly evangelizing to their students (e.g., God can still find an alternative route to saving that person's soul), Mei Lin often uses this concept to talk about how this belief allows her to be very bold, direct, and honest about who God is and why people should follow Him, even if it means that person feels hurt by her comments. She's okay with speaking what she considers to be unpopular truths because she trusts that God can turn that hurt to good.[6] It also means that she believes that if she gets in trouble for talking about her religious beliefs in ways that might cross the line of professional expectations for public school teachers, God can turn that to good as well.

As a result of this belief, Mei Lin is generally a very open and frank personality. She doesn't shrink from saying what she thinks or why. As an undergraduate, this sometimes put her in conflict with classmates and professors who disagreed strongly with her viewpoints. As a result, she's wary of university professors in general, whom she views as most likely not Christian. All our interviews begin slowly, as Mei tends to be suspicious of my motives and my questions before she warms to the topic of her faith. Her passion for the subject and the fact that I am an interested listener always seem to overcome her initial wariness by the third or fourth question. There are times, in fact, when she breaks from the pattern of interviewer and interviewee to ask about my own spiritual well-being, what is holding me back from salvation, whether I think I might find my way back to God—a break in the pattern that simultaneously amuses and jars me.

Moments of Hesitation—Being Responsible to a Higher Law

As part of my classroom tour, Mei shows me her reward center, which is a set of stacked drawers behind her desk. It's the place where kids come to choose a reward when they have earned enough points on the classroom management app Mei uses to track their behavior. She slides open one drawer to reveal a neatly ordered display of Oreo packs. She points out the pens shaped like cacti and carrots—"The kids love these pens! And they were so cheap to get!" There is a drawer filled with office supplies and a crate filled with chip bags. Mei created this system to reward students' behavior, in part, because she doesn't believe in tying effort to grades. Grades are reserved for mastery, but effort can earn you points for the reward center. I ask what the most popular item is. "They love food," she says. "They almost always choose food."

As a Christian, Mei feels a strong responsibility to care for her students' physical and educational needs. She takes seriously the call in the Bible to feed the hungry and clothe the naked. She recounts a story of a 21-year-old student who was aging out of the school system but needed one semester of her class to qualify for his diploma. "He had a lot riding on his shoulders. His father got cancer, so he had to take care of his father and when his father died, obviously he had to provide for his mother and his two sisters." Mei has sympathy for this situation because, as she says, his frequent school absences and inability to finish school aren't "because of his own shortcoming—it's because of life. I mean, we could say it's because of what God did, giving his father cancer and all that." Mei explains that he would leave work to come to school for just 1 hour a day for her class and then go straight back to work again. He started coming less and less, so Mei had a conversation with him to see what was going on with him:

> He told me that he is in a lot of credit card debt. He's working to try to pay it off and that's why he can't attend school. It was $2000 in debt. He knows I'm a Christian and he used to be a Christian until his dad got cancer and he understandably fell away. I just said, "Hey, between us. Here's what I'm going to do. You can go home and talk to your mom if you want, but I'm willing to give you $2000 and you can take it knowing that I'm not going to ask for any of it back, first, because I could lose my job—you just can't give students that much money, right?—But second, you can trust me because you know I'm a Christian and I believe that Jesus gave up His life for me. $2000 compared to that is nothing and all the money that I have is from God anyway. I feel God calling me to give you this money because you need it to do something that's right for yourself and your family."

Although Mei told the student that he didn't need to pay it back, he did pay it back after he graduated. The important part of this story for Mei isn't necessarily what happened with the student—if he paid it off or not, if he goes on to college or not—it's that she aligned herself with her God's laws instead of the ethics of the school system. Although she says that this incident is "something massively on my conscience," she is at peace because she knows that "as a Christian I did the right thing." Over and over as Mei tells me stories like this one, where she prioritizes her Christian ethics of care over what she perceives as the ethics of her job, she talks about her fear of losing her job, but she is always derisive about her own fear. The job, she says, is only hers because God gave it to her, so if she loses it doing

God's work, she can expect that God will take care of her and bless her for her obedience.

Not every situation plays out in this way for Mei. "I made this decision pretty easily," she says. "It was pretty obvious to me it was the right thing to do. And this is just money." Mei's fear of losing her job causes her to make other decisions in more complicated circumstances. She has a homeless student whom she thinks about inviting to live with her family, but she can't figure out how to make that scenario work without getting caught:

> It got uncomfortable in my head thinking, "How does he get to school? Does he Uber? Do I drive him and drop him off a block away from school so no one sees us together?" That's when I realized that was weird . . . it's just so much messier.

For Mei, giving a student money outright is less complicated (and less likely to get her fired) than having a student live with her.

To be clear, Mei's fear of being fired really bothers her. She sees that fear as a manifestation of a lack of faith, not as a reasonable response to a situation that has complicated ethical concerns. She wonders aloud,

> Why would I believe God will protect me from the money being found out but I don't believe God will protect me from having a kid living at my house being found out? So am I really putting faith in God or am I putting faith in the situation being easy or difficult to hide?

Mei's moment of hesitation here isn't that she finds these ethical situations murky or difficult to navigate—she always feels confident that she knows what the right thing is to do. What she finds difficult about these situations is her own unwillingness to follow God's laws no matter what the consequences might be. "I kind of refuse to think about it, because I know the right thing I should have done and I didn't do it. I think that is [a] sin." The problem is that while Mei feels that Christian ethics are "healthy" and make her feel like she's doing the right thing, "teacher ethics" make her feel "handcuffed" and unable to care for kids in meaningful ways. Where she finds joy in submitting to God's laws, she's "not submitting happily to [teacher ethics]."

The place where Mei sees the most conflict between God's laws and teacher ethics is in the area of evangelism. Her spiritual call to teaching is an explicit call to evangelize. She takes no small amount of pride in the ways in which she is able to stealthily insert evangelism in her curriculum and her interactions with students. During her first year of teaching, she assigned students to write a personal narrative and then wrote her own to use as a model for students to learn from. She wrote about her relationship with her father and then drew parallels between that relationship and the relationship she has with God. "I mean, I did not need to include the God part," she tells me. "I threw that in there because I want them to know I'm a Christian. I want them to get the Gospel." She is untroubled by her knowledge that a lot of her students "might have been uncomfortable." One student came back and asked her if she was allowed to talk about God in a public school classroom. She says, "I immediately responded with, 'Yes, because this is not me trying to evangelize you,' but . . ."

I break in: "You're really aware that you are sliding [the God part] in there to evangelize but you're going to say that it's not?"

She laughs. "Of course. They can't prove it"—she pauses for a quick beat and then eyes me and my recording device suspiciously—"unless they get ahold of this recording. But then I can sue you for something, right?"

"Sure," I say, and she laughs again. I ask her if she's had trouble this year with the personal narrative, but she says that she decided not to use the personal narrative again because she doesn't want to "have to spend some time explaining it away," even though she thinks she could explain it away.

I ask for clarification: "So, it seems to me that you're thinking about how you need to evangelize, but you're also thinking that in order to keep evangelizing you're going to need to toe some lines so that you can continue evangelizing without getting fired. Right?"

Mei puts her hand to her chin and says,

> I think one of my [spiritual] mentors did say something like that because I was struggling with not evangelizing. I completely forgot, but that's a good point. That's definitely something I can use to make myself feel better when I don't evangelize as much as I want to.

She points at me and amends quickly: "I don't think there's really ever a justification for not evangelizing." For Mei, there's never an option or an argument that is going to make her feel better about not fulfilling her evangelical call. Anything less than explicit, verbalized evangelism is a cop-out, a sin, a reflection of her human inability to trust God.

Moments of Hesitation—The Cost of Public School Teaching

Mei sees a vast gulf between the nature of the work of teaching in a public school and the work of showing forth God's love to others. Some of this is because Mei's definition of evangelism doesn't allow a "soft" version of evangelism that might occur just by being a happy and kind example of a Christian. Some of this is because Mei's call to teaching came attached with a very specific plan to go abroad, teach English, and evangelize in countries where Christianity is still a minority religion—none of which included teaching at a public school in the Deep South. Mei's change of plans regarding her teaching career is something she is still trying to come to terms with. But just as important as the other two factors, Mei talks about the way that working as a public school teacher has damaged her own spirituality. Her relationship with God has suffered; her trust in Him (and His trust in her) has faltered as she passes up opportunity after opportunity to spread the Gospel because of the constraints of her job. There is a real sense of sadness from her as she talks about the way that she feels herself slipping spiritually.

Part of her grief over who she sees herself becoming is centered in the idea that she can't even properly repent of the spiritual slips she is making every day as a public school teacher:

> Whenever I actively ignore opportunities or I don't stand up for God the way I think I should, I want to repent and apologize and change my ways. But then I knew I couldn't repent because the next time it happened I would do exactly what I did the first time.

For Mei, her sense of repentance involves turning from sin and performing a new version of obedience when presented with a similar situation in the future. However, her desire to keep her job keeps her from true repentance.

"I've gotten to the point where I don't even say, 'Sorry, God,' anymore; I just say, 'Look, this is the way it is now.'" Mei's eyes fill with tears that she blinks back quickly. "When you disobey and you know you're disobeying and you actively disobey—it's a very unhealthy thing for your spiritual walk. And now I've been doing this for three years and right now, I'm in a very weak spot spiritually."

Mei's concern isn't just idle guilt: She has real concerns about her salvation. She's worried that her struggle to stand up for God and boldly evangelize might be a sign that she was never saved in the first place. "I'm panicked because I think I'm not saved, and this whole time [I thought I was saved] I was just faking it or something or lying to myself." Here, we might come to the crux of Mei's discomfort with being a public school teacher who doesn't take every opportunity to evangelize. Mei's anguish might be less about whether the students in her classes hear the word of God and are saved and more about her doubts about her own salvation.

Mei feels a pull between the two discourses she feels herself straddling in her religious spheres as well. In a blog post that she writes for me[7] titled *Learning to Check My Christian Discourse at the Door* she reflects on an incident that happened while she was teaching Sunday school at her church. She saw a little boy purposefully take something from a little girl and she "lost [her] mind" because she felt it was such a clear instance of bullying:

> I brought the boy out, and the conversation went something like:
>
> [Mei to the boy]: Why did you do [that]? What were you hoping to do?
>
> [Boy]: I don't know.
>
> [Mei to the girl]: How did you feel when he did this to you?
>
> [Girl]: I feel bad.
>
> [Mei to the boy]: I need you to change. Are you a man or not? A man who steals candy from little girls? Does that sound manly to you? No?
>
> When I was saying all of that, someone walked by with a side comment of "Ooooh, you're a bad boy," and that was when I remembered the Gospel and said, "Jesus died for bad boys."

What bothers Mei the most here isn't that she responded with anger (although she does feel bad about that because she considers yelling to be a sinful response to a problem). Instead, she's bothered by how quickly she used what she views as a secular approach to discipline—an approach that she sees as behavior-based instead of Gospel-based. It isn't until someone else walks by and makes a comment that she remembers that her church space disciplines differently than her school space. She reflects:

> Before [teaching at a] public [school], my teaching experiences have been primarily in openly Christian contexts. The encouraged discourse of discipline is grace-centered. A language and attitude of grace is afforded to all. . . . [What I should have said was] "Jesus loved and stood up for women and children, and He teaches His disciples to do the same. Your behavior does not demonstrate the teachings of Jesus. You've sinned, but Jesus died for your sins, so this shouldn't be on your heart as guilt, but Jesus also set you free from sin, so you must change." To the girl, the dialogue should go something like, "Do you forgive him? He sinned against you and hurt you, and Jesus knows how that feels because people hurt him too. But Jesus died for them and forgave them, just like he's forgiven you. Can you rely on Jesus to give you the power to forgive others?"

Mei contrasts her conception of an *ideal* response—a response that centers Christ's love and forgiveness, as well as the call to change, implicit within that love with her actual response—a response that she finds to be "empty and man-centered":[8]

> I appealed to manhood without basis on the Bible and [I also used] shame ("You wanna be the man who steals candy from little girls?"). I appealed to a code of conduct: "We don't do things like bullying," and man-made kindness: "Can you forgive him?" without basing my response on the Gospel. In my mind, I wasn't a Christian mentor; I was a feminist public school teacher: I can't have an older boy get away with "teasing" a little girl. Not because it's against God but because it's against feminist values.

What Mei is horrified by here is how quickly and automatically she reverted to her teacher identity, with secular approaches to behavior and discipline. It can be argued, of course, that Mei (and the other participants) never fully use secular approaches because they are so steeped in discursive figurations of teacher as Christ, but Mei often uses these terms herself to juxtapose two separate options in her choice-making process. Particularly, she frames the tensions that she feels as binary (i.e., here's what my religious identity says I should do and here's what the secular world is telling me I should do instead). It isn't that the secular view always runs counter to the religious view (both Mei's education professors and her religious leaders agree that yelling at kids isn't optimal disciplinary practice); it's simply that for participants like Mei, it's dishonest and disloyal to God to not give Him the glory for these actions.

Mei's experience in her Sunday School class solidifies her growing unease with who she is becoming as a result of being a public school teacher. Mei sums up her big takeaway in this way:

> I hate public schools. I've gained a new set of values and dialogue as a public school teacher; school policy is the Bible I fall back on for authority. . . . Behavior changes, but the heart remains the same, and that behavioral change does not carry over into the next day or the next classroom. And [the language of public dialogue has] permeated into my Christian spaces. I'm a Sunday school teacher, and I couldn't bring myself to use Gospel-centered language in my church classroom.

Already annoyed by the way that being a public school teacher has forced her to curtail her evangelism, Mei is disgusted to realize that even in her Christian spaces she is using what she can only categorize as secular values and discourse. It's one thing to feel like she has to check her Christian identity at the door of her public school classroom (she does feel that way, although I read her performance of teacher as being deeply embedded in Christian practices). It's entirely another to realize that she has gotten so numbed to the difference between godly discipline and secular discipline that she uses secular logic even in a religious space.

Moments of Hesitation—The Question of Affirming

Even as an undergraduate, Mei Lin grappled with how she might show acceptance and love to people in the LGBTQ+ community while still communicating her belief that God views anything other than heterosexual, married sex as sin. She attended her university's training, sponsored by the LGBTQ+ resource center, on how to create safe classroom spaces for members of the LGBTQ+ community. She spent a great deal of time with fellow Christians in her cohort considering what it meant to *love* someone versus what it meant to *accept* someone, particularly around issues of gender and sexuality. What she keeps coming back to over and over, no matter how much training or how many conversations she has, is that there is no way she can condone or approve of the gender and sexual identities of the LGBTQ+ community. The pull that she feels is a little different than the pull that Noelle navigates with her transgender student. Noelle has mastered the sidestep, preferring to avoid the issue unless she can carefully phrase her words so that she doesn't give offense or so that she can be read in multiple ways. Mei Lin sometimes feels offense and pain can be godly.

What the training and conversations have done is made Mei deeply aware of the damage that the LGBTQ+ community feels has been done to their personal identities as a result of heteronormativity. I ask her if she feels her training made her more sensitive to what it means to identify as LGBTQ+. "Yes," she says definitively. "It made me realize how damaging heteronormativity is and how much we do need more representation. Like, for people to feel recognized and acknowledged in their identities. But the thing is, I don't want them to feel reinforced in their identities." The difference, for Mei, is easy: It's okay to acknowledge that there might be people who are gay, but it's not okay for them to feel like God's okay with that identity. She continues: "Like, I know that it feels bad to see only straight people in movies, but I don't want to see gay people in movies. Unless it's a Christian movie where Christians control the narrative and they become not gay."

I give a sound that might be interpreted as either an affirmative or a negative, and she rushes to fill the gap: "I know that's not cool for people who are identified as LGBTQ+ and they go through like conversion therapy and all that. That would be terrible. But I will still want that instead of reinforcing that identity. Even though I know it hurts people." Mei knows there is violence (in a Derridean sense) whichever way she turns in this situation. There's the violence and the damage that are caused by not affirming identities—a violence that "hurts" and might even be a "terrible" violence. Thanks to her training and research on the subject, Mei understands that

LGBTQ+-identifying students are more likely to commit suicide—something she directly ties to homophobia, transphobia, and heteronormativity. It's not that Mei is ignorant of the hurt that "rejecting a part of someone's identity" might cause. She knows and she enacts the violence anyway.

What makes this choice to enact a violence possible, of course, are Mei's religious beliefs, particularly her beliefs around heaven and hell. Mei's belief that gayness is a sin causes her to consider affirming queer identities as an eternal violence, and she's choosing to play the long game. Hell looms large, and she reasons that if she *truly* loves someone, in the Christian sense, the best thing she can do now is hurt them in the short term by telling them the truth about how God views their sin. She talks about how she herself is disciplined by God, that there are parts of her personality and identity that he hates just as much as he hates gayness. She explains: "You know, I'm very sarcastic, and I think God rejects that, too. And that's an important part of my identity." Perhaps Mei's perspective is best expressed by the Bible itself when it states that "no chastening for the present seemeth to be joyous, but grievous: nevertheless afterward it yieldeth the peaceable fruit of righteousness" (Hebrews 12:11, King James Version). Mei can acknowledge that God's rejection of gayness might feel grievous, but that doesn't mean that the pain of the chastening isn't worthwhile if it can be turned to righteousness.

It's helpful to understand that Mei eschews pop-culture representations of hell, where the devil is the king and gets to run the show. Hell is just as much a manifestation of God's power and love as heaven is. She views hell as a very literal place, with genuine suffering, wrath, and punishment, but all that punishment and suffering glorify God. Because Mei's goal as a Christian is to glorify God, to acknowledge his glory wherever she sees it, she talks about how even if there is someone in hell who she genuinely loves but who was not a Christian ("I put my grandma in that position," she confesses), she can't do anything but consider that person's punishment as just. From her own Calvinist perspective,[9] she can't do anything else but view the punishment of that person as a source of God's glory. In all instances, God's glory is meant to be joyful. The glory of God's punishment can be just as joyful and glorious as God's mercy and grace. Certainly, this belief finds its way into her classroom practice in sometimes unexpected ways (see Figure 5.3).

I ask about the wall decorations—
full of posters about
Romanticism,
Finding Concrete Details to Support Your Essay,
Overviews of Ethos, Pathos, and Logos—
I notice, I say, that you haven't put up inspirational quotes
like I see in other teacher classrooms.

No kittens
urging students to "Hold On"
while clinging desperately midair to a rope;
no chunky block letters
declaring there's no such thing as failure
as long as you keep trying;
No quotes from Albus Dumbledore
reminding students that their choices determine who they are,
not their abilities.

She grins—points to a poster next to the clock—
"Here are my inspirational quotes!"
It reads: Hell is empty, and all the devils are here.
A nod to William Shakespeare, a black poster
With devil red horns setting off the print,
Next to the clock, ticking down the seconds
and minutes until the bell.

A single desk sits beneath the poster.
"This is where I sit kids who aren't working very hard."

She laughs
and invites me to share the joke.

Figure 5.3: *A Portrait in Poetry: Mei Lin*

When the subject of LGBTQ+ issues comes up outside of school, Mei views it as her responsibility to affirm what she knows about God: that all sin is repugnant to him and being gay is a sin. If that hurts the people she's talking to, she believes that God's sovereignty can turn that hurt to good by opening up guilt, which leads to change. This stance is very much influenced by Mei's understanding of Christian love and by her own experiences with being convicted by the Spirit to change and turn away from sin.

In a classroom setting, Mei's approach is a little less direct than it is in her personal interactions outside of school. She talks about how she purposefully avoids addressing LGBTQ+ issues in her planned curriculum:

> In my mind, I knew *Hamilton* would have been a great example to talk about LGBTQ+ issues, because some people love to think about how John Lawrence and Alexander Hamilton had a thing . . . but I was like, "Nope, I'm not going that direction because no one's going to think it's weird that I don't go in that direction."

It's not that Mei doesn't want to share her opinion and her belief; she does. But she's worried that even opening space for the conversation might be seen as a way of affirming LGBTQ+ identities, and she can't risk it.

However, specifically because she is a Christian, Mei feels a responsibility to show how one might behave as a Christian in what she views as a non-hateful way, even toward those who are sinning. Because of this, she does tell kids in her classroom to stop using the term *gay* as an insult, although her attempts are sometimes rather uneven. She says:

> If there are two boys being touchy or whatever, I'm just like, "Oh, you guys really like to be close together, don't you?" And they will say, "What? No! Not gay!" And then, that's when them knowing I'm a Christian is really helpful because that's when I step in and say, "Don't make gay an insult." I want Christians to leave my classroom knowing that they can't have that way of thinking or interacting with LGBT people. Just because you're a Christian doesn't mean you have to hate them or be insulting or view them with that much negativity.

Mei wants to model for Christian students the ways that you might be a Christian and not be hateful or insulting toward people who identify as LGBTQ+. What she doesn't seem to notice within this example is the way that her own assumptions about gender norms (and discomfort with gayness) come through in her original statement ("Oh, you guys really like to be close together, don't you?"), which she says with a joking tone but which I read as a way of regulating both masculinity and heteronormativity. In short, she sets the students up to make a homophobic comment (by denying her reading of their behavior as gay) and then chides them for doing so. It's only the chiding that she self-identifies as a religiously informed understanding of how she interacts with students around LGBTQ+ issues in the classroom; I identify her first statement as being equally religiously informed.

Looking Forward

As Mei finishes her third year of teaching, there are big changes in the works. She's returning for her fourth year of teaching in her same school with a similar teaching load, but she has big plans to make her original calling of teaching ESOL (English for Speakers of Other Languages) abroad a possibility. She has always wanted to return to China, but with the current climate for Christians in China, her parents have worried that it would be unsafe for her to return as a Chinese citizen. Mei had been putting off making a decision about whether to apply for U.S. citizenship because she wasn't sure if that was what God wanted her to do, but her mom finally made the decision for her and sent off her application on her behalf. Mei expressed relief that her mother took the decision out of her hands because now she can move forward without so much indecision. If she can teach and live abroad as an American citizen, Mei is aware of the additional protection she will be afforded. That protection means she could more openly evangelize, which has always been the end goal for her calling as a teacher.

Discussion

Mei's religious identity is unique among the participants in several interesting ways—some of which might be attributed to the discursive figurations that are unique to Chinese Christian and Chinese American Christian religious traditions, but some of which might also be attributed to her personal sense of herself as an "extreme thinker" who is all or nothing when it comes to the way she frames herself and the world around her. Evangelism is one of Mei's all-or-nothing propositions, and because her job as a public school teacher limits Mei's ability to evangelize, Mei believes that her identity as a teacher is often in direct conflict with her identity as a Christian. Important findings from the portraits of Mei can be summarized as follows:

1. Evangelism is a guiding principle for Mei as a teacher and as a person. Mei's practice as a teacher, from the models she writes for students to the financial support she offers, is framed by Mei as specifically Christian-informed practices.

2. Mei consistently finds her teacher identity to be damaging to her relationship with God. Mei centers evangelism as being key to the way

that she shows God she loves and trusts him. Because Mei cannot view evangelism as anything other than speaking (as opposed to the softer evangelism of Mallory and Noelle, which can include just being happy or kind), whenever Mei misses an opportunity to evangelize, she feels she has lost some of God's trust in her. Additionally, Mei feels anger over the way her public school teacher identity has bled into her practice as a Sunday school teacher.

3. Mei's beliefs around God's characteristics deeply influence the way she views her own interactions with students. Because Mei views God's love as being as much about correction and calling out sin as being about kindness and gentleness, Mei often views classroom discipline and student interactions with the same lens. She counts on God's ability to turn all things to good to make interactions in which she hurts people's feelings into a powerful evangelical experience, especially if she believes she is just speaking God's truth. This is particularly crystallized thinking around Mei's beliefs and interactions with students around LGBTQ+ issues.

Mei is also unique in her own positioning of herself in public school systems. Where both Mallory and Noelle often position themselves, from a Derridean hospitality view, as the hosts of their classrooms (including their ability to set the limits of the hospitality they offer to students), Mei positions herself as simultaneously a host (to her own students) and as the other (as a Christian within a public school system). As an other, she perceives herself as not receiving an unconditional welcome and is often asked to "speak [a] language, in all the sense of this term, in all its possible extensions" (Derrida, 1997/2000, p. 15) that she cannot, in good conscience, within the bounds of her own religious discourses, speak. In short, Mei is very attuned to the violences—and the accompanying personal anguish—offered to her as a Christian in a public school setting, but she is less attuned to the violences she offers to others in the same setting.

As I worked through how to write a portrait of Mei that is both critical and generous, the poststructural conception of discourse became even more important to the study. So, yes, Mei can be read as a problematic evangelical teacher, if we choose to read her that way (there are instances in which I cannot read her any other way based on my own assumptions and ways of being and knowing). But to create a complicating and complicated portrait of Mei, the discursive figurations that make her ways of being and knowing commonsensical and inherently intelligible (to herself and her religious community) have to be explored and understood, particularly the discourse around love. Mei enacts specific violences *because* she sees these moments as acts of love—a violent love, a hurtful love, and a shame-inducing love—because that is what her conception of love entails. She is loved by God, and that love often causes her to feel shame, to feel hurt, to feel inadequate, to feel *rejected*. Ultimately, this love pushes her to become something different, something that within her discourse is viewed as infinitely better and more worthy of love. She can't imagine (nor does she want to imagine) a love for her students that doesn't encompass these same qualities. Although it seems like an impossibility, Mei's determination of who is a "being who is not" (Derrida, 1997/2000, p. 5) or a being who is excluded from a hospitable welcome is framed by her as an act of love. Refusing to offer hospitality sometimes feels to Mei like the only way she can highlight for the other the behaviors and actions that are unacceptable within her discourse.

Mei's discourse around love and Christian sacrifice makes some of her most generous moments possible as well, including her loan of thousands of dollars to a student so that he can finish his diploma. She gives up her own lunch when students go hungry, and it's important to her that she gives up *her* lunch instead of sharing snacks she has bought as rewards for the class. While it's important that kids don't go hungry, it means more if she makes a personal sacrifice—especially so she might be able to say, "Hey, this is my lunch, but I'm going to give it to you because I've been given so much through Jesus, and I know he wants me to share that with you." Her willingness to push against the limits of hospitality that educators might offer to students as prescribed by her district is possible within her performance of Christian teacher, a performance that she is happiest with when she prioritizes her religious beliefs over professional strictures. In certain instances (like loaning a student money), Mei's personal and religious definitions of hospitality are broader and perhaps less limited than the public school system's definition of hospitality. However, the bounds of Mei's welcome to the other often come attached to a commitment by the other to be evangelized, to be addressed by her, to be seen by her, and to be welcomed by her as part of an evangelical tradition instead of a tradition of hospitality.

Notes

1. What Mei's leveled and linear system of teaching rhetoric might ignore is that most youth already come to class primed with the *ability* to argue. They may lack the academic definitions of the words that describe the kinds of rhetorical moves they already make instinctively as experienced consumers and producers of language.

2. In our interviews, Mei never attributes her religious beliefs and practice to her Chinese culture and heritage, and it is beyond the scope of the current study to do so. However, I personally wonder if some of Mei's beliefs about the central role of evangelism in her faith are influenced by the fact that the Christian tradition in China is tied so closely to 18th-century European missionaries. The state of Christianity in China today is more tenuous because of governmental crackdowns on religious practice, a fact that Mei is well aware of and that influences her desire to return to China as an English-language teacher. She not only sees a great need for evangelism, but she also understands that returning as a Chinese citizen who doesn't have the protection of the U.S. government could put her at real risk.

3. Here, a review of the Five Points of Calvinism might be helpful, as represented through the TULIP acronym: T—Total Depravity, U—Unconditional Election, L—Limited Atonement, I—Irresistible Grace, and P—Perseverance of the Saint.

4. This is a book in the New Testament.

5. Paul is the apostle credited with writing several books in the New Testament.

6. This was a conversation that grew quite heated between Mallory and Mei, where Mallory argued that to knowingly inflict pain because you trust God to make it better is an irresponsible stance for a Christian and a public school teacher. This conversation was the impetus to Mallory's reflection (discussed in the following chapter) of how her definition of love is shifting to account for a performance of love that feels like love to the person who receives it.

7. Mei Lin chose to write blogs instead of recording herself on Flipgrid as part of her reflection process.

8. When Mei talks about "man-centered," she is not critiquing this response as being centered in a failure to perform a certain form of masculinity (although her response does have some of that in it as well!); instead, she is commenting that the response centers itself in the logic of humankind (fallen and weak) instead of in the love of God.

9. I had originally written "Christian perspective" here, but Mei corrected this during her read-through of the chapter: "I might say 'Calvinist' because this is almost certainly rejected in most Christian circles. Even some Calvinists would say that's going too far. I base this largely on Revelation 17–19, especially Rev. 19. Heaven rejoicing and glorifying God because he's violently judged Babylon (a symbol for sin)." What might be worth noting here is Mei's awareness of the ways that her thinking on this topic might be at odds with other Christian perspectives that do not attend to Calvinist principles.

References

Derrida, J. (2000) *Of hospitality: Anne Dufourmantelle invites Jacques Derrida to respond* (R. Bowlby, Trans.). Stanford University Press. (Original work published 1997)

Feige, K. (Producer), & Coogler, R. (Director). (2018). *Black panther* [Film]. Buena Vista.

Miranda, L. (2016). Hamilton: An American musical. In J. McCarter (Ed.), *Hamilton: The revolution* (pp. 23–26). Grand Central Publishing.

CHAPTER SIX

Portraits of Mallory: Individual Ministries

MALLORY DONALDSON[1] IS A big personality, something she admits almost apologetically. "I've always been like this," she says, "Like, I can run a room, no problem." She can, too. In her undergraduate classes, she was always the focal point, the funny one, the outspoken one, the loud one. It's no surprise that even though she graduated from different cohorts than the other participants in the study, at our first focus group both of them said, "Hey, I know you!" She's outgoing and friendly, and she's a gift in group settings because she knows how to put people at ease, ask them questions about themselves, and get the conversation flowing. She's a funny mix of self-promoting and self-deprecating, too: "Polish Perfect!"[2] she'll respond laughingly if you ask her where these social skills come from, as if a yearlong course on etiquette and dinner manners can take all the credit for what's clearly a natural way with people.

As a teacher, she's jumped right into running a room. Classroom management has given her very little trouble. Her quick sense of humor and fondness for the absurd make her a favorite among the high schoolers—mostly juniors—she teaches. She's just as likely to head off a potential conflict with a quip and a shared laugh as with a more serious conversation in the hallway—although she feels comfortable doing both. It's not just people skills that set her apart, either. Even though she's only a second-year teacher, she's been asked to head up her grade-level curriculum team to rewrite curriculum, provide leadership in team meetings, and get everyone on the same page. In the fall, she coaches volleyball, and it won't take too much coaxing for her to tell you that she was a *very good* high school volleyball player, such a good high school volleyball player that she still holds multiple records at the private Christian high school she attended, thank you very much. She brings all this experience into the classroom—people skills, leadership and planning skills, and coaching skills—and combines it with her deep love of literature.

The reason that Mallory is half apologetic about her ability to run a room has a lot to do with the education she received at her private Christian high school. "Girls weren't supposed to be, well, this *much*," she says. "Like, we were supposed to be quiet, and be kind in like a very sweet, submissive way. My teachers spent a lot of time telling me that I needed to be a little bit less—or a lot less." "Running a room," the phrase Mallory uses to describe her strong leadership skills and innate charisma, was something that only men should want to do. Mallory spent a lot of her high school life trying to fit herself into the tiny box of what the people around her felt a woman should be. By the time I met her, as a senior in college, Mallory was trying to figure out how to build a bigger box to contain her own changing conceptions of what she could and couldn't be as a woman, as a Christian, and as a teacher.

Mallory's religious identity is tightly bound with her identity as a daughter and a sister. Religion, she'll say wryly, is the family business. Her father is one of the founders of a local megachurch; her mother taught at Christian private schools while also performing the many unpaid responsibilities that often fall to pastors' wives in the Deep South. Her brother, a recent graduate from a very conservative seminary, is an assistant pastor in a neighboring state; her sister is a producer and media specialist at one of the campuses of her father's church. She attended a private Christian school from kindergarten through 12th grade, participating in multiple weekly Bible studies, praying in every class, being mentored by teachers and older students, serving as a mentor to younger students, and working with her peers as an accountability partner[3] or a Bible study leader all along the way. On Sundays, it was typical for her to be at church all day, working in the children's ministry during one service and attending her own worship service later. "I remember finding out [as a teenager] that people had religion and it wasn't everything, which was really surprising to me. Like, every conversation I had ended with 'We'll pray about it.' It was our version of 'Okay, love you, bye.'" Attending church is never just about attending church or just about hearing the weekly message, it's also about supporting her family and supporting her parents. Church, religion, and faith are the air that she's breathed her whole life, but lately, she's started to feel a little suffocated, particularly when she considers the discursive constructions of femininity and womanhood in Christianity.

It's not just that Mallory wants to be able to run a room in peace without judgment about her failure to perform Biblical visions of womanhood. It's also that she's been profoundly let down by religious responses to sexual assaults—her own, in college, for starters, where the emphasis of those around her was not on holding *him* accountable but on *her* giving forgiveness to her attacker. She's also uncomfortable with the glossed-over sexual assaults of young women in Christian schools, in Christian families, and in Christian churches. She relates one particularly difficult incident from a job at a church that she held when she was in college where she was in charge of organizing baptisms. She was instructed to let a young man who had sexually assaulted his sister get baptized because he deserved grace like any sinner,[4] all while the church provided virtually no support for the young woman who had experienced the assault. It might be fair to say that Mallory's exit from regular church attendance (during her first year of teaching) was deeply tied into the ways that she saw forgiveness and absolution for men being paid for by the suffering and silencing of women.

Mallory's religious identity is very complicated. Although she no longer attends church, excising the influence of religious thinking from her daily life would be impossible. Her language continues to show religious influences—she talks about what it means to show God's love in her teaching only a few sentences after she confesses that she probably doesn't believe in God anymore. A recent social media post features a picture of her with two robed graduates (students she taught last year who are now graduating), and the caption reads, "I will forever be grateful for the grace they showed me every single day as a first-year teacher." It's not just the use of religious words and phrasing, either. Sometimes Mallory and I find ourselves arguing points of doctrine from our respective former faiths' perspectives (issues of priesthood authority or the sanctity of the Bible as the only source of truth) with far too much passion for people who no longer believe there's a point to arguing doctrine. Mallory confesses to being very confused by her own identity, particularly when she feels herself sliding into what she can only view as moral relativism. "Like, how am I even making decisions anymore?" she wonders, as she talks about how unmoored her own decisions feel from anything solid.

Mallory's religious beliefs are divided in her head into two spaces: things she was taught at her school and things she was taught at her father's church. While both spaces identified as nondenominational, Mallory identifies her home church as having come out of the Southern Baptist tradition but being "a lot less formal." Her school taught a variety of denominational beliefs, but what sets it apart for Mallory is the emphasis on legalism:

> Like, you were graded on if you could say a verse and you got a point off for every time you missed a word. And we'd keep logs for how often we prayed and we got awards for how many nice things we did for people.

The problem for Mallory is that legalism became a way of quantifying righteousness and faith, and in her home church, they "always said that you couldn't do that." During high school, Mallory would keep journals that marked how long she could go without sinning—an exercise that she enjoyed until she realized her pride in how long she could go was itself a sin.

Mallory's understanding of God's will is tied to her understanding of God's love. Because God loves her, he has a deep interest in her life, in her choices, and in her relationships. Mallory's responsibility then was to always discern what God wanted her to be doing, to continuously keep herself "in God's will." Mallory received mixed messages about what it meant to stay in God's will. Mallory's dad taught her that "God's will wasn't a tightrope stretched over the Grand Canyon. God's will *was* the Grand Canyon and you had to try really hard to climb out of it." What Mallory learned from her parents was that God's will was wide and deep and that there was plenty of space in God's will for any individual choices she might make. But she also was taught that God had a deep interest in the choices in her life, particularly in her school spaces, which sometimes complicated her understanding of her own agency. "I mean, when I pledged at a sorority, I remember crying because I was like I don't know if God wants me to pledge to this sorority or that sorority," she says with the disarming laugh that often hides the underlying anxiety she feels. "It was a really ambiguous or really arbitrary line of where we drew the line of what God cared about and what he didn't." I comment that a lot of people find a lot of comfort in viewing God as always interested in their lives, but that it seems that for Mallory it became a source of anxiety, "Yes," she affirms, "because everything was like, 'Did you pray about it and did you get an answer about it?' That can be paralyzing because you cannot be sure what the answer is." What might be most important from this, is that Mallory believed and generally continues to believe that there is *an* answer—a right thing to do in every situation. If she can figure out what that one right thing is, her path will be smoothed in front of her.

Mallory absolutely became a teacher because she felt spiritually called to the work as a way to glorify God. She says of that initial call:

> I was in high school and I was at a spiritual retreat. I was crying and I think we were supposed to be praying about where we're going next or what our purpose was in God's kingdom . . . and there was a song where the chorus says, "Oh, to be like you God. I'd give all I have just to know you. Oh, to be like you, that others may feel your love." And I thought about my English teacher who was just so loving and so kind. . . . She never talked to me about God, she never told me what I had to do. And that was honestly when I decided that I could teach public school and never talk about God. . . . I could just love my kids so well that at the end of the day, they would wonder what that is.

Mallory's call to teach is bound up in her own sense of being loved by teachers and how that love helped her to understand more fully the love that God had for her. Importantly, her decision to teach in public school instead of private school hinged on an understanding that she could still do God's work and show God's love to others even if she couldn't talk explicitly about her belief.

I ask her why she felt called to teach language arts, specifically. Why not math or science? She points to the walls of her classroom, draped in large pictures of famous authors such as F. Scott Fitzgerald and Emily Dickinson:

> There is something about English class for me that it was, it was just easier for me to see God's love and grace in books. . . . I really connected to God

> with books—like an odd amount probably. I remember reading *The Great Gatsby* [Fitzgerald, 1925]. It was a very religious experience. I have tons of journal entries that are quotes from *The Great Gatsby* and then me writing about what it taught me about God and human nature.

(See Figure 6.1, a picture of Mallory's classroom window, decorated with the classic literary symbol of God's watchfulness—T. J. Eckleburg's eyes. Gatsby and Fitzgerald have a prominent role in the decorations in Mallory's classroom.) Literature became a conduit to greater understandings about God, in part because her own English teachers framed them that way within the context of a Christian education. When the class read *A Tale of Two Cities* (Dickens, 1859/2014), it wasn't a reading that was primarily framed as a historical novel; instead, they used the novel to talk about religious concepts like sinning and sacrificial love.

Figure 6.1.

However, language arts classes were also a place of very literal physical and emotional safety for Mallory, too. In a school where the lines of professionalism and relationships between kids and adults were often blurred uncomfortably,[5] Mallory recalls walking into English classes where the teachers tended to be more professional and more liberal and thinking: "Thank

God. I just feel so safe here, I feel so connected here, and I feel I have a place here." That feeling of safety, connection, and acceptance felt very sacred to Mallory, and she says "making other kids feel that way" was a big part of her call to teaching language arts, specifically.

Mallory's ambivalence toward religion and God now have complicated her thinking around how she teaches, why she teaches, and who she is as a teacher. Because so much of the reason she went into teaching was based on her spiritual call, she has had to do some careful thinking about what teaching might look like now for her. She's holding on to her conception of English class as a place of community, as a place where kids feel loved and connected to the teacher and to the other kids in the room. She actively continues to use the religious concept of grace to frame the interactions she has with kids in her classroom. But she's trying to let go of some of the things that made her Christian education problematic: "the wildly inappropriate" closeness of teachers to students, the way that love sometimes meant shaming kids, particularly around issues of sex and gender.

Perhaps most important, Mallory's conception of love is shifting and being reshaped. What she previously considered to be love now feels inadequate. She says,

> We were taught the love of God was basically, "I accept you. I love you completely and I love you too much to let you be the way you are." It's like you're completely accepted and loved and I want you to be so much more.

As a child and as a teenager, for Mallory, this meant that teachers, peers, and fellow churchgoers might approach her and tell her she was doing something wrong to hold her accountable to her Christian faith. That calling out was recognized by her and those around her as being love. In Mallory's tradition, Christians have a responsibility to keep each other in God's will. "Basically," Mallory says,

> if you love someone and you see them doing something that you think is wrong—even something like, I prayed about it for you and I don't think you should go to this university—if you feel that way and you don't say something to them. . . . That's not love; that's harm.

As she moves into classroom spaces, she's working to challenge a definition of love that only accounts for the intention of the person who bestows love ("I love you too much to accept you how you are") and is trying to perform a version of love that insists that an integral piece of giving love is that it is received *as* love—that the person who is being loved picks up the action as kindness, love, acceptance, and respect. In our focus group, she explains this shift to Noelle and Mei:

> I feel like so much of what I grew up with and what I hear in the Christian circles I run in is about showing love, and we do so much talking about how we show love and so little thinking about whether or not someone *felt* loved. And I get that's not necessarily what Christianity calls for us. But for me, being a teacher, it matters to me how my kids are picking things up. There are ways I could hold up my religious views to my kids and still say I was showing love in the way love was defined for me, but I know my kids would not feel loved.

Teaching in a public high school hasn't necessarily required Mallory to reorient her conception of love. Instead, leaving her church has opened for Mallory new ways of thinking about love, of defining love for herself, even while she acknowledges that so much of what she knows about love she learned through religion. That new definition of love has opened new performances of love in every space of her life, including the classroom.

Mallory is keenly aware that there can be a disconnect between what she had been taught was an expression of love (correcting others) and how she wants students to *feel* inside her classroom (safe, accepted, and respected). This disconnect is particularly true for Mallory as she considers how she treats students who identify as LGBTQ+. "I don't think there's a way to 'correct' LGBTQ+ students without them feeling rejected, and I see a disconnect in those two things. For me, the way I made peace with that is that I am gay-affirming." Mallory's gay-affirming stance stands in stark contrast to the other participants in the focus group conversation, who both are concerned that they have a responsibility as Christians to accurately represent God's stance on being gay (God loves gay people because he loves all people, but being gay is a sin) to their students. What might make the difference between these beliefs is that while Noelle and Mei continue to be deeply informed by Christian conceptions of love that primarily consider the intent of the person who gives love, Mallory has embraced a conception of love that accounts for how the person who receives love feels. This shift in belief allows for a different performance of love for Mallory in classroom settings.

Mallory teaches in a diverse school in a suburb of a busy metropolitan area. The school itself is tucked into a quiet neighborhood, across the street from an elementary school and from a sprawling county-maintained park with a pond, baseball fields, and trails through wooded areas. The school is perched on the edge of a large master-planned pool-and-tennis community with neat but aging houses lining the curving streets edged with tidy lawns. This high school is zoned in a way that takes in both prosperous pool-and-tennis communities and communities packed with rows of trailer parks. Most of the planned communities were built during the housing boom of the 1990s, but there are just as many streets in the area that are still flanked by tiny houses built during the post–World War II housing crisis on little plots of land divided with chain-link fences.

Although the school itself is genuinely diverse in terms of race (almost equally divided between Black, White, and Hispanic students with a slightly smaller Asian and Pacific Islander population) and economic status, Mallory's classrooms often do not feel as diverse as the general population due to the school's tracking policies (policies that mirror the majority of school system's tracking policies). If you attend Mallory's class during one of the classes that has been tracked as Honors, there is a notable difference in the racial makeup of the students compared to one of her on-level courses, something that Mallory attributes to racism in educational policy and practice. She *thinks* she might have convinced the administration to let her try a few sections of untracked English 11 in the future. She's worked hard for the opportunity, engaging administrators in multiple conversations in which she pointed out not only the vast racial inequity of the tracking system but also the complicated literacy work that her on-level students have engaged with through her class.

As a teacher, Mallory has high standards for herself and for the teachers around her. Her greatest annoyance as a team lead is when she perceives other teachers as not fulfilling the demands of the job adequately. She believes that teachers should plan effectively to build engaging units while also building strong interpersonal relationships with kids so that they feel comfortable and safe in classrooms. One of her department chairs asked her why she got so annoyed when other teachers said things in meetings like "Oh, my kids can't do this! We're not going to be able to do that unit/assessment/text." Mallory explains that what annoys her about comments like these is that a good teacher should be able to say, "My kids can't do this *right now*. I'm going to need to do this and this and this with them before we can do that." She has a certain amount of disdain for teachers who write kids off, don't believe in them, or don't attempt to understand them.

Mallory has high standards for kids, too, but her level of annoyance when they don't meet those standards is considerably lower than with adults. She happily defines what a good teacher is, what good assessment is, and what good instruction looks like but balks at defining what a good student is (See Figure 6.2). I ask her why she feels uncomfortable with the label of "good student" but not the label of "good teacher."

I ask, "How do you define a good student?"
She scans my face because
she suspects
I don't really want
an answer to that question.
There's a silence in the recording
Here
as she weighs what she should say.
She looks at me with a question
In her eyes,
Can I challenge the question?
I nod her forward.
The silence in the recording.
The two beats of unspoken negotiating.
Laid bare
Here
She plunges in:
"I don't super like the term good student,"
She says, "just because
I think it implies there are
bad students."
You can't hear my nod of approval
Here
in the silence of the recording.

Figure 6.2: *Portrait in Poetry: The Silence in the Recording*

She draws deep distinctions between adults and children:

> I know that adults are still changing and growing too, but I just think it is ridiculous to put labels on teenagers. Like they're changing so much and they're growing so much. And we have so much power, so the minute you label them "bad" that has detrimental effects. Whereas when I label the teacher down the hall "bad," it is not going to have the same effects because we are all grown. Like, self-actualizing people. When you're an adult, yes, you change, but you're just not as malleable.

Mallory has a great deal of patience and grace for teenagers because she considers them as in process. They can be forgiven for making mistakes and for not understanding how to treat each other because they are still learning. Adults, however, are not given the same grace. Mallory holds herself and her colleagues to a much higher standard, particularly in the way that they talk about and treat students. Some of this, of course, comes from her religiously informed beliefs about what it means to be a teacher, which is "to put others' needs and wants before yours . . . or servant leadership."

But it is also possible that some of Mallory's construction of the young people in her classroom as fundamentally different from her adult peers comes from her experience within mentoring relationships within church and school spaces. In all of Mallory's Christian spaces, mentoring was an important part of her religious experience, and even as a high schooler, she had multiple mentors and simultaneously mentored younger classmates. There's a big difference in the performance of the role of mentee and mentor. Mallory explains that when she is the mentee, she feels free to admit to faults, to be open not only about her struggles with faith but also about broader struggles in general. Where she might call out her peers and tell them that they weren't in God's path with a sense of showing forth God's love, she would most likely hesitate before calling out a mentor (and that hesitance would increase with the age difference). Particularly as a teenager in her school setting, there was a sense of currency in having some kind of struggle to talk about with your mentor, and Mallory recalls that she was always really hard on herself when she was with her mentors. When Mallory worked with younger students as a mentor,[6] she recalls that she worked really hard to appear as someone who had it all figured out or who was more mature, particularly about spiritual issues. As a mentor, she was far less judgmental than she would be with her peers; she wanted to assure her mentees that they were loved by God, give good advice, and assure them that their mistakes were normal and could be learning experiences. In short, she might give her mentee guidance, but the overall feeling she wanted her mentees to have within their mentoring relationship was a feeling that there was a space for them—in church, in worship, and in God's love—regardless of what choices they were currently making.

As a teacher, then, Mallory has much higher expectations of performance for her adult teacher peers because she positions herself as a peer in those spaces. As a peer, Mallory's evangelical Christian discursive figurations allow her to position herself with her colleagues as someone who can see their faults and insist that they do better. For the young people in her classroom, Mallory positions herself much more as a mentor figure. When Mallory is in a mentor role, she is much more tolerant of mistakes (even repeated mistakes). Although she will correct students, she just has much less frustration when they don't live up to her expectations. Mallory's favorite mentors in high school and college were the mentors who encouraged her to be less judgmental of her own inability to be perfect, who assured her that she was going to turn out just fine, or, better, who laughed when she confessed to a sin and made her take herself less seriously. It's no surprise, then, that when Mallory positions herself as a mentor she also positions herself as someone who doesn't believe there are "bad kids." For Mallory, there are just "good kids" who need someone to believe in them, to be patient with them while they are learning, and to give them encouraging guidance.

As an early-career teacher, Mallory has been most surprised by "all the different stories and situations" that she sees as she connects with kids. Because she attended a private Christian school, her understanding of high school and high schoolers "is worlds different from what I thought it would be." This is not to say that this has been an unwelcome surprise. Mallory explains that while it's fun to find kids who are very similar to her, particularly personality-wise or humor-wise, she finds "just as much fulfillment on the other side a lot of times." Where Mallory had imagined herself being a teacher who would educate kids to help them become the kind of person she is (and was), she views her work differently now. As she has teased apart what it might mean to teach in a public school, where not everyone shares the same religious framework, she has decided that her job is to help kids become who they want to be and to help them figure out how to engage responsibly with other people.

The kids Mallory most easily connects with or, at least, the kids she feels the most drawn toward are the kids "with a little bit of attitude" or "kids who are really witty and quick." She thrives off the verbal repartee that can happen with teenagers. Whereas some teachers are intimidated by teenagers' barbed sarcasm and mostly good-natured ribbing, Mallory has harnessed this playful stance to build a classroom where kids are able to be linguistically playful while they talk about literature. She gives as good as she gets, and the kids know that if they dish it, they have to be able to take it, too. Mallory also confesses that she thinks a lot about the complicated and very real lives the kids in her classroom are living outside of school. Because kids trust her and because she reads their writing, she knows more about kids than other teachers might. She doesn't know everything, but what she does know reminds her that the kids she teaches are growing up with vastly different lives than she did. She has kids whose parents are being deported for being underdocumented, kids with parents in jail, and kids who are living in foster care because of familial sexual abuse. It isn't that Mallory's upbringing was free from problems, but what strikes her is how very *adult* these problems are that her kids are facing.

Moments of Hesitation—Revealing a Christian Identity

Mallory's moments of hesitation—the places and instances where she feels pulled by her religious identity in uncomfortable ways—most often reflect the ways in which she is grappling with that religious identity herself. The majority of Mallory's moments of hesitation were classroom incidences in which students aligned themselves (sometimes in ways that increased their vulnerability in a peer space) with Christianity and seemed to be looking for affirmation or recognition from Mallory. Revealing her own Christian identity, especially when she is currently trying to figure out exactly what that identity means for her in private spaces, is a source of anxiety for Mallory. Equally anxious are the instances in which she feels she has to make a choice between issues of equity and social justice and Christian values as she teaches her course. Some of this is because Mallory is intimately aware of the politically conservative leanings of most evangelical Christian communities (including her home church, her private high school, and her own family sphere), which set up the work she does around White privilege, feminism, and representation as liberal nonsense. Always, she is intimately familiar with how what she says will be picked up by Christian kids in the room and how their interpretation of what she says might lead them to feel unsafe, unloved, or unaccepted.

She recounts one such instance where a group of kids were speculating about her weekend plans. One kid said, "Oh, she's going to go out and party." Another girl responded, "She wouldn't do that. She's Christian." She was uneasy with the incident for several reasons: first, because all the kids turned to look at her to see if she would verify that she was or wasn't Christian. She felt very literally saved by the bell when the class period ended at that exact moment. But more uneasy for her was the notion that she had been read as Christian. It's not that kids don't ask her if she's religious—they do, all the time. "That is never as odd for me as that moment of her just feeling that she knew that I was Christian." I ask her why that bothers her when part of her initial call to teaching included the idea that she wanted her students to feel God's love from her so strongly that they would want to know why at the end of the day. She thinks for a moment and then says,

> I do think a part of it is that since I attended a Christian school, I am always trying to keep in mind that I cannot teach the way I was taught. . . . So in those moments it makes me think I'm not doing so well at that. Like, I thought that I was doing so well being neutral, and apparently I was not.

Mallory flips easily in and out of the language of secular teaching and Christian-informed teaching, reflecting the ways in which her own identity is still in flux. While she refuses the label of evangelism to describe her teaching, she is much more comfortable stating her goal as showing Christ's love, even as she balks at her students identifying her as a Christian in general. For Mallory, the distinction is in definitions. If she were to evangelize, she would be putting forth the Gospel and trying to influence kids' religious beliefs. However, she believes she can show Christ's love by making someone feel accepted, wanted, and enjoyed. Showing forth the love of Christ is still compatible with the new worldview Mallory is forging: She still believes firmly that her role as a teacher—whether she uses the language of her teacher education course work or the language of her religious framework to argue it—is to make kids feel loved, accepted, and enjoyed.

Mallory, too, is torn by how Christian identities are picked up by others in the room. While she says that it isn't important to her that people think she is *not* a Christian, she still says that she left that incident feeling like she should pull a few kids aside to say something like, "Hey, when you talk to me, I want you to know I'm not judging you or listening to you with a Christian filter." She is specifically talking about Arturo, a boy in her class whom she describes as being "so marginalized from most teachers." She and Arturo have a strong relationship, and she felt for a brief moment when he looked over at her he was doing some recalculating about everything he knew about her. "I would just hate it if that recalculation were, 'Oh, she's been judging me this whole time,'" she says, "I mean, he has a kid. He has a 2-year-old and he shows me pictures of her every day. I was just really aware that I wanted him to know how much I enjoy him." I point out that she seems to be thinking about the assumptions other people might make about Christians. She agrees and says, "I just think he would assume that Christians would not be okay with him having a child outside of marriage and getting a girlfriend pregnant when he was 17." What Mallory is thinking about in these moments isn't necessarily about her own comfort (although she does feel uncomfortable), it's more about how her religious or not-so-religious-anymore identity might influence her relationships with the students in her classroom.

Mallory has purposefully leveraged her religious insider status in other instances to strengthen her relationships with students. Another moment of hesitation she reflects on is her interaction with a student named Joel whom she had previously struggled to connect with. He came to school wearing a shirt from a program that was from her home church, her father's church. In other instances, with other kids, Mallory would have completely ignored the shirt. But with Joel, with their relationship being a little tenuous, she made a different choice. "I just have known that we have had a rough go for a while," she says of the moment, "so then I was like, 'Oh, hey, you're in the Aspire program? Do you go to that church?' And he was like 'Yeah.'"

Even in this simple and short exchange, which took place in the chaos of the beginning of a class period, Mallory was aware that she was presenting a version of herself that Joel could identify with and connect with. Mallory's leveraging of her religious insider identity paid off in this instance. Her perception of her relationship with the student is that they are doing better now "probably because he reads me as Christian now."

Even though her leveraging paid off, Mallory has some regrets about using that identity, too, and not just because she no longer feels like it's an accurate representation of who she is *right now*. Some of it is that she has committed herself to a different set of ethics to Joel as a fellow Christian than she feels she has with other students. She believes that he watches her more closely and more critically to see the way that she performs her Christian identity as a teacher:

> He had already read me as a liberal, probably not Christian . . . but then we have this moment where I'm like, "I'm on your team. I know your church. I'm from your church." So then now [he'll always be looking at how I talk about ethical and moral issues wondering,] "Are you going to stand up for your church when Christianity comes up?" And I know he's thinking that because I definitely did that when I was in college. Like, once I knew a teacher was Christian, I would think, "What are they gonna do?"

Mallory's assumptions about the way that the student is reading her now that she's disclosed a Christian identity stem from her own performance of Christian student in her public university setting.

Mallory's concern over this complication of her teaching identity caused her to perform teacher differently moving forward. During a reading conference with Kaitlyn, a nonreligious student who was reading *The Poet X* (Acevedo, 2018) as part of her independent reading,[7] Mallory was "super aware" that Joel was listening in from his desk to hear what she would say when Kaitlyn asked, "Is religion really this crazy? Is this what it's like to grow up in religion?" In that moment, Mallory felt a split in her responsibility—feeling responsible to identify with Kaitlyn *and* Joel in the exact moment. I ask her how she decided to respond, and she shakes her head derisively at her own decision. "I just said something like, 'Oh, this character obviously feels that way. And religion is such a broad term." Mallory feels uncomfortable with her response to this because it feels like a dishonest answer, a refusal to grapple with something that her students want to discuss. She's also uncomfortable with her response because she's aware that she responded differently than she normally would because Joel now reads her as a Christian. I ask her if some of her response was a way of trying to make everything more comfortable for herself:

> No, I actually felt what I chose to do was *more* uncomfortable for everyone. I felt like I would have felt more comfortable if I had just been a human in that moment and said, "Well, listen, yeah, I grew up similarly; I felt that reading this whole thing. It is rough, huh?" But that would have jeopardized my relationship with Joel. So I stayed in like this weird [place], like I was very awkward and not the way I like to be with students. And I could tell Kaitlyn was wondering why I wasn't talking to her about it. I guess I made the choice to stay in discomfort.

What's most interesting here is how much pressure Mallory feels to present a version of herself as a Christian because she has identified herself as one to Joel. There are many, many instances, for example, in which Mallory is fine with being read as a liberal, as a non-Christian, or, at least, as a liberal but religiously impartial figure. However, once she has identified herself to a student as having a religious identity, her anxiety ratchets up over performing a certain version of teacher for him.

Moments of Hesitation—Grappling With Sexual Assault

Mallory sits with her arms wrapped around herself, her fingers pressing deeply into the flesh of her upper arm. When she gets this anxious, she is unaware of how hard she is pushing, or perhaps she is anchoring herself with the physical pressure. I know from previous experience that she will bruise herself if I don't intervene, so I lean over and almost apologetically uncurl her fingers. She gives a half-smile—an acknowledgment that I caught her—and firmly presses her hands together in her lap. "This one's a tough one for me," she admits. She begins the rhythmic finger tapping that always accompanies anxious thinking for her: thumb to pointer, thumb to middle, thumb to ring, a double tap of the thumb to pinky, thumb to ring, thumb to middle, double tap on the thumb to pointer, over and over and over and over and over again, back and forth, and she starts to talk slowly:

> I have a student, like on the football team and we've had these moments—one, like I knew he had been abused, right? He had written that early on and we had talked about that. And he had seen his father abuse his mother, right? All of this is like through his writing, right? But he's like everything you would think of when you think of a football player, right? He did not know how to show his emotions, but he came to me and was like, "I don't know how to ask you this, but I'm not okay. There's something I have to talk about and I don't want to tell anyone here." And I was like, okay, we'll get you therapy. And we did, right? And then he gave me a Christmas gift and a really sweet letter that was really short and super appropriate. He's very good at boundaries. But he wrote me a little letter that was like, "I've never had a teacher care so much about my emotional well-being. I just want you to know that it meant a lot to me and thank you so much. And I'm becoming a better man and thank you," right? And I've kept an eye on him because he's been struggling.

Mallory looks at her hands again, picking at the perfect manicure she maintains to keep from biting her nails. The finger tapping resumes.

> He asked to talk to me in the hall again this week. And he was like, "I have something and I so don't want to ask it. Especially of you." And I was like, "Okay, we can talk about what's happening." And he said, "I'm going to court tomorrow and I need a character reference."

Mallory nods and leans forward, speaking more quickly now:

> And I was like, of course, of course, I'll write you a character reference. And honestly, in my head, there was not even a doubt. Like maybe he stole something. It's not even a hard thing for me to think that this is a good kid who made a stupid mistake, right? He said thank you and all that stuff, but then he was like, "I need you to know what it was about." Then he started crying and he was like, "It's for sexual assault." And then he just kept

> crying and saying he was so sorry and he said, "I did it. And I'm pleading guilty. It's not whether or not I did it. It's just about what happens next." And I was just listening and he said, "I want to be a different person. But I'm scared. I don't know if I'm going to get to be a different person." It was so sad. I said that I was going to have to think it through, and then I asked if I could give him a hug. And I did hug him and I told him that there are always choices—that no matter what happens in court, you still have a choice of who you are going to be the next day. Then I told him that he was a good person, but I will say, in my head I wasn't sure about that. But I knew it was what he needed to hear.

Mallory cocks her head sideways a little and spreads her hands flat on the table in front of her. "So then I was just trying to decide if I was going to write it or if I was going to tell him that I couldn't." What's unspoken here in the interview between Mallory and myself is the fact that we both know this is a big fucking deal to her—that if the kid had stolen something, she wouldn't have had a problem writing a letter singing his praises but that sexual assault changes things for her. It's not just that sex has long been a taboo subject, but it's also bringing to the front her personal history with sexual assault and the forgiveness her religious discourse has taught her that women are expected to offer to rapists and sex offenders. It's further complicating the strict moral judgments she has in place to make sense of her own sexual assault:

> I have a very, very strict line on what I think is a good person and a bad person. And sexual assault crosses over that line for me. I still can't say he was a bad kid. But I don't know if I can say that he's a good kid.

I let a few beats pass. We sit in silence for a minute, the unspoken history we both know but won't acknowledge sitting in between us. I cough a little and then say, "So let's talk about what makes this an aporia or a moment of hesitation for you. What makes this undecidable?" She talks through all the steps that she took to try to make the best possible decision: She has visited the counselors and assistant principals to see if they know if the girl goes to their school, is in her classes, or is on her volleyball team. She talks to several trusted teacher friends:

> I went to people for advice, and every single person was like, this is impossible. I don't know. . . . And what I just kept coming down to was, "What can I do that's right? Like what can I do that doesn't do anything wrong?"

She concluded, after all this input and soul searching, that there was no exactly right decision and that she would have to just make the decision that she could live with. The anguish with which she tells the story suggests that there might not be a decision that she can comfortably live with.

What's pulling at Mallory here, more even than the undecidability of the decision, the absence of a clearly right or clearly wrong answer, is the issue of responsibility. She can't stop thinking about her responsibility: as a teacher of a kid who needs support, as a feminist who has decided that she wants to support and believe women, and as a Christian who has been taught to offer forgiveness and grace. She walks me through each of these responsibilities, as we unpack this moment of hesitation together:

> Part of [my hesitation around writing the character reference] was that there's another girl somewhere that I feel responsible to. I was watching my female students throughout the day, and I just kept thinking, *What if I found out it was her?* It would change everything. If I had a face connected to this girl, it would change everything. I started to feel like it could be any of them, right? And women are already so not believed, or there's a situation just like this where it's like he did it, but he's a good kid. I've held this one belief that I'll always support girls.

What Mallory finds she's coming up against again and again are two beliefs that feel pretty sacred to her: first, that she's the kind of teacher who advocates for kids who have it rough and, second, that women and girls who are sexually assaulted deserve justice.

I ask her why this particular decision felt like a place where her religious identity and her teacher identity were in conflict. To me it felt like this might be just one of the many ethical issues that all teachers face in the course of being a teacher, regardless of religion. Mallory shakes her head emphatically when I suggest this:

> No, what was coming from my Christian identity was the forgiveness aspect. My Christian belief made me feel like I should write for him, right?

> That's where the pull was. Forgiveness, grace, redemption. All sin is the same, right? Like, I was about to write for him when I thought it was stealing—I had no qualms until he told me what it was. That was the part where I felt my religion tied into it a ton. Who gets grace and who doesn't get grace? Who gets protection and who doesn't get protection?

At least part of Mallory's hesitation here stems from her own experiences as a survivor of sexual assault and the way that her sexual assault was talked about in religious spaces. What was very clear to her in that space was that no one, absolutely no one, wanted to do the difficult work of supporting a sexual assault victim through the legal and emotional aspects of the assault. Instead, she was consistently told that she would only feel better if she let it go, gave it to Christ, stopped being angry, forgave her attacker, and moved on. Here, because she is the trusted teacher of a young man who *is* an attacker, she is being asked to become complicit in the discourse that she found so damaging during her own experience. In short, she's being asked to write a letter asking the judge to forgive this kid, consider his future, contextualize his own background as an extenuating circumstance, all things that infuriated her when she was on the other side of the experience. And yet, she can't *not* contextualize her decision with regard to this kid. She can't erase what she viewed as his sincere remorse, his anguish over his own actions, and his understanding that he did something very wrong.

"So did you write it?" I ask, although I'm sure I already know the answer.

"Yes," she says.

"What did you say?"

> Well, I rewrote it like 85 times. I still don't feel good. I basically said I can only speak to what I've seen in my classroom. I cannot speak to the way he handles himself with women. But I can say that I put him next to shy kids because he's so good at talking with people. I ask him to partner up with kids who are new. I highlight his name when substitutes come in and stuff like that. He's so good with everyone. He just is very thoughtful and kind—

She breaks off suddenly and gives a small shudder as her face twists into a brief, very brief, expression of revulsion before she straightens her features again.

I observe as neutrally as possible, "You just had a very physical reaction to saying that."

"Yeah. Because I can't . . . Like, [sexual assault's] not kind. That's not what kindness is." She shakes her head clear of whatever she's thinking and continues speaking immediately:

> So then there was a part of my letter that basically said, "I know he did this thing. I know his background and situation. I originally had a line that was like, I ask that you keep his future in mind, but I took it out. It felt too much like Brock Turner's dad.[8] Like I . . . I read that and I wanted to throw up. So I took that part out and the part about his situation. I left in that he had admitted this transgression to me. I have seen his remorse firsthand. I'm aware that his actions carry consequences for everyone involved. And I just left it at that.

Mallory's revulsion with the whole situation, with being in the same situation as Brock Turner's father, with being positioned as an ally of someone who assaults women sexually is only tempered by her belief that every kid deserves to have someone, and this kid literally had no one else to speak on his behalf. Two factors settle her decision to write a letter on the student's behalf: first, her recurring thought that this kid didn't have anyone and, second, her belief that the student is engaging in a repentance-like process:

> I saw the depression, I saw the regret, I saw the guilt as he started learning what [sexual assault] meant. And a lot of that was tied to discussions we had in my class. We were talking about sexual assault and hitting these things so hard. It was killing him probably.

Although Mallory would theoretically challenge repentance and forgiveness narratives in sexual assault, her language makes it clear that religious figurations around repentance still influence the way she makes choices in the classroom. It's important to her that the student professes regret, that he takes ownership of his mistake, and that he is willing to face consequences to try to make it right—all steps that coincide with Christian conceptions of repentance. It's equally interesting that Mallory uses the word *transgres-*

sion—a word with strong religious ties—within her letter to describe the sexual assault. I read this in two ways: first, as evidence that Mallory is using her religious framework to make sense of the situation, including positioning herself as a woman who might be able to offer forgiveness to a man. But second, I see it as a way of softening the sexual assault for herself *and* for the intended audience. The word *transgression* could cover a multitude of sins (including the stealing that she would so easily have written a letter about) and avoiding naming the transgression as sexual assault makes the letter (and the choice to write it) easier to live with. Furthermore, the use of the word *transgression* appeals to religiously informed constructions of repentance for the judge who will read it as well. In some ways, Mallory's use of the word *transgression* may work to remind the judge that all sin is the same and that religious forgiveness is offered to all who ask for it. Mallory's natural talent for considering audience and purpose (in this case, the audience for the letter is most likely a White, male, Christian judge and the purpose of her letter is to make clear that this student is a more complex person than the charge against him) as a key part of her communication style may also account for the religious word choice.

Mallory's moments of hesitation highlight how religion and religious discursive figurations linger and shape teacher practice even though the teacher themselves may be actively working to question these discursive figurations. But Mallory's moments of hesitation also highlight how new performances of welcoming in the other become possible and thinkable when highly regulatory discourses (like the discourse of her school around gender and sexuality) are loosened up, examined critically, and reworked.

Looking Forward

As Mallory looks to the future, she's excited for her third year of teaching. This next year she has several goals for herself: She wants to continue advocating against a version of school that continuously labels kids without accounting for its own racist assumptions in that labeling. In her role as a grade curriculum leader, she wants to professionally advocate against the implementation of tests meant to get kids ready for tests meant to get them ready for more tests. She's applied for graduate school, too, where she'll work toward a master's degree while teaching full-time. Next year, she has plans to rework her final unit to include space for kids to independently research the inequalities that they see in their school and community and present their findings to school administrators with recommendations for how to improve their school. She's comfortable with the teacher identity she's created for herself—one whereby she is seen by the vast majority of kids as someone who really likes them, who can joke with them, but who has firm boundaries and expectations for them.

Discussion

Like Noelle, Mallory sees the work of teaching as being compatible with a Christian worldview. As Mallory has opened herself to other discursive possibilities around womanhood, sex, and gender—largely from a feminist standpoint—she has found her Christian background and identity to be both sources of strength and places of personal frustration. Some of the major themes from Mallory's portraits include the following:

1. Mallory credits her religious identity with many of the interpersonal skills that make her a responsive and student-centered teacher. She learned in religious spaces what it meant to care for kids, to love them, to be patient with them, and to forgive them when they make mistakes. She equally learned how to hold kids to high standards of behavior and academic excellence from her religious schooling. Mallory attended a church that focused on developing leadership qualities, and she has felt well prepared for the leadership roles she has been asked to take on as an early career teacher. All of these are qualities that she sees as assets to her classroom identity and that she ties directly to her religious identity.

2. Mallory's religious identity is in flux, and these shifts open up new performances for her as a teacher. As she shifts her sense of what it means to accept or love, she is moving to a classroom practice that reflects her sense that kids should *feel* loved, not just *be* loved.

3. Although Mallory is actively trying to push against discursive figurations that insist that women should always be gentle, quiet, and forgiving and that boys will be boys and they can't control their sexual urges—she sometimes finds the sheer work of pushing against these dis-

courses exhausting. However, because she has pushed against certain discursive formations of her religious identity, other issues that are very anxiety-inducing for other participants do not seem to affect Mallory as powerfully—for example, she is the only participant who identifies herself as LGBTQ+-affirming.

4. Mallory's religious upbringing has made her hyper-aware of the standards she is being judged by and the ways in which her current performance of teacher might fall short of Christian students' expectations of a fellow Christian. The majority of the moments of hesitation that Mallory self-identified were centered on how her Christian students felt, how they read her, and what they assumed they knew about her.

Mallory's performance of teacher is still deeply influenced by her religious identity, even as she has anxiety about her religious identity becoming known to her students. It's not that she is particularly private or doesn't want students to know things about her, but she feels like they might make assumptions about her that she is uncomfortable with, and this discomfort is with both religious and nonreligious students. For her religious students, she is concerned that they will be more critical of her, especially as she talks about things like sex, gender, or social justice issues from a more liberal perspective than her evangelical Christian discourse would have made possible. Or, alternately, she worries that if she explains that she no longer attends church, they will feel like she is uncaring or resentful of their religiously informed ways of being. For her nonreligious students, she is concerned that they will assume she is judging them from a Christian framework. When she shares the name of the private Christian school she went to, she worries that students (both religious and nonreligious) will assume things about her that are no longer true for her. She doesn't, however, feel it's appropriate to share her full religious journey with students as a public school teacher.

From a Derridean hospitality perspective, Mallory is attempting to open up her performance of hospitality in the hope that she can offer unlimited hospitality to all the students in her class. This is easier in one-on-one situations in which Mallory can adjust her performance of teacher—her language, her way of being, and her humor to mirror the particular student in front of her. Hospitality, we might consider, is an act for individuals—a contract of welcome and generosity between a host and an other or, at the very least, a group of others who arrive together, speak the same language, and share the same version of otherness. The limits of hospitality may stretch when one is faced with multiple others, with multiple forms of otherness, multiple languages, and multiple expectations of welcome. And it's this stretching of the limits of hospitality that Derrida is so interested in—the places where historic notions of hospitality break down or seem insufficient are the exact places where a new performance of hospitality might offer itself up. Mallory's discomfort then, with her own religious identity, might be read as discomfort with the ways in which her religious identity limits her ability to unconditionally welcome the other. It should be noted, however, that she is equally discomforted by the ways in which her teacher identity—fairly liberal and progressive—*also* limits her ability to unconditionally welcome an entirely different other. Either way, Mallory is always keenly attuned to the aporias of hospitality and the limits of unconditional welcome in her classroom interactions with students.

Mallory's complex thinking about ethical dilemmas and the role her religious identity plays in those choices reflect her own recalibration of belief about who is a being who counts and who is a "being that is not" (Derrida, 1997/2000, p. 5). Her understanding and awareness of these shifts are clear in her language to fellow evangelical teachers: "I get that's not necessarily what Christianity calls for us," she notes as she explains that she is choosing to show forth a version of love in her classroom that will be recognized by students as love. She is purposefully rejecting some of the previous calibrations she made about who is a being and who is a being that is not that were directly influenced by her Christian understanding of love. While this recalibration opens up possibilities like being LGBTQ+-affirming, it is worth noting that there are still places where Mallory comes up against the limits of her hospitality and grapples with how she will decide the recipients of hospitality. This is particularly true when she considers what it means to support students (who, for Mallory, are still learning and growing and becoming who they will be) who, through their actions, ask Mallory to recalibrate her understandings of sexual assault, forgiveness, and responsibility. To be clear, Mallory's move to generously welcome in the other—even when the other is someone who admits to a sexual assault—did not come without personal anguish over whether it was the right choice or whether she should do something differently. Instead, Mallory made a choice after carefully weighing the impossibility of the decision, contextualizing the situation to account for multiple understandings of the situation, considering who and what she was privileging in her choice, and recognizing that a choice had to be made. It is, perhaps, the clearest example of how all of the conditions of an ethical decision might be met, and yet the decision still might have a quality of uncertainty, due to the aporia of decidability. Whichever way Mallory chose, violence *and* hospitality could be claimed by someone as a result of her decision. This intertwining of violence and hospitality is perhaps what Derrida refers to when he speaks of offering an unlimited welcome while maintaining power; it is certainly a key attribute of why this decision felt so impossible to Mallory herself.

While a rejection of a certain set of values and beliefs might mean that Mallory feels unmoored when making decisions (she notes, "How am I even making decisions anymore?"), Mallory still clearly considers the limits of what it means to be a "good person" or a "good teacher." In fact, of all the participants, Mallory is generally the most finely attuned to the aporias that she faces as a public school teacher. Her always-in-progress examination of her own religious identity and beliefs and her moves to challenge some of her religious beliefs and ways of being make space for her to sit with the aporias of welcoming in the other and making impossible decisions in her classroom with more complexity than was possible for other participants.

Notes

1. It's important to acknowledge in this portrait, particularly, my own relationship with Mallory. Although I taught Mallory in a Teaching Reading to Adolescents class during her undergraduate experience, our relationship has become much more complex. As part of a very complicated placement situation, Mallory needed additional support during her student-teaching experience and often turned to me as an advocate. After her graduation, Mallory has become less of a former student to me and more of a friend, sometimes a daughter, sometimes a colleague. I know a great deal more about Mallory—on and off the record—than I do any of the other participants. In some ways, this both simplifies and complicates this portrait: I feel more sure that I am interpreting Mallory's intentions generously, but I am also a strong influence on Mallory's attitudes about teaching, youth, feminism, love, religion, relationships, and so on. It is very likely that this portrait reveals as much about the portraitist as it does about the portrait.

2. Polish Perfect (a pseudonym) is a popular etiquette program for children from Grades 6 to 12. In the program, youth learn social etiquette with the intent of developing leadership skills.

3. The term *accountability partners* refers to friends or peers who agree to work together to hold each other accountable, most generally in terms of sexual purity. For example, a person might call their accountability partner before they go on a date so they can review appropriate physical boundaries.
4. I had originally written "he needed the forgiveness" here, which reflected my own Mormon perspective of baptism as a literal washing away of sin. During her member check, Mallory gently corrected me and reminded me that in her belief system, baptism is largely symbolic. She suggested the change in phrasing to "he deserved grace like any sinner" to more accurately reflect the language that might be used in her religious spaces when talking about baptism.
5. A few examples to illustrate my meaning here: Mallory recalls an assembly where all the girls were brought together and the wearing of jeggings was banned "because it was distracting the male teachers." The overfamiliarity wasn't just confined to male teachers, either: Mallory recalls instances in which female teachers overshared details of their own sexual lives and prompted students to talk to them about what they were doing sexually as part of the mentoring relationship. No wonder then that the Language Arts Department, most of whom maintained more stringent teacher–student boundaries as a product of having worked in public schools, felt like a haven of emotional safety.
6. Mallory was paired with a student who was 2 years younger in a mentoring relationship during high school; in college, she served as a youth group leader for 10 to 20 teenaged girls in the role of mentor. Throughout all her high school and college years, she also had multiple mentors with whom she met regularly.
7. *The Poet X* (Acevedo, 2018) details the adolescence of a Dominican Catholic teenager in ways that often present religion from a troubling perspective. For example, the main character's mother punishes her by having her kneel on rice in of front a picture of the Virgin Mary when she goes on a date with a boy.
8. Brock Turner's dad is a reference to a letter written by the father of Brock Turner, a Stanford University swimmer whose rape and sexual assault case garnered national attention, largely for the judge's lenient sentencing of 6 months of probation. Brock Turner's dad's letter argued that his son shouldn't serve prison time for "twenty minutes of action" and urged the judge to consider his son's bright future as part of his sentencing.

References

Acevedo, E. (2018). *The poet X*. HarperTeen.

Derrida, J. (2000) *Of hospitality: Anne Dufourmantelle invites Jacques Derrida to respond* (R. Bowlby, Trans.). Stanford University Press. (Original work published 1997)

Dickens, C. (2014). *A tale of two cities*. Black & White Classics. (Original work published 1859)

Fitzgerald, F. S. (1925). *The great Gatsby*. Scribner.

PART III

Group Portraits

ALTHOUGH THE INDIVIDUAL PORTRAITS of each evangelical teacher include data drawn from our focus groups, the multiplicity of portraits would not be complete without a group portrait: a chapter that examines who we were when we were together and what we said when we made sense of religious and teacher identities as a group instead of as interviewer and interviewee.

The focus groups themselves were conducted at the beginning and end of the research study. Although all the portraits blend time and space, the individual portraits provide a fairly cohesive narrative examination of each individual teacher, their religious beliefs, classroom practices, and moments of hesitation. This was much harder to accomplish with the portraits from the focus groups, which exist separately in two very different time periods in the study. The first half of Chapter 7, which provides a portrait from the first focus group, makes plain the tentativeness of the beginning of a new study: Participants deferred to me as the researcher, they waited for me to guide the conversation and ask the questions, and they were careful about the topics they chose to engage in and how they interacted with each other and with me. It is worth keeping in mind that before we reconvened for the final focus group, when we unpacked common tensions and hesitations in their teaching experiences throughout the study, all the participants had participated in three interviews with me and had engaged in multiple personal reflections about their religious and professional identities, moments of hesitation, and the ethics of their classroom and personal decisions.

The time jump is evident in Chapter 7, as the second half of the focus group portraits reflect more confidence on the part of the participants to challenge the thinking of other participants, introduce their own topics, and ask questions of each other. Because each participant had already been engaged in their own inquiry into the moments of hesitation they were experiencing as evangelical Christian teachers in public school classrooms, our second focus group felt different to me: more raw, more honest, more vulnerable.

Some of this increased familiarity and depth of discussion, too, come because of the affordances of talking about these issues with other evangelical Christian teachers. Conversing with others who had similar religious and teaching experiences allowed participants to use a shorthand of terminology and ideology not present in their conversations with me, a former Mormon. In our individual interviews, it was very common for me to say things like "Can you tell me what you mean by that term? I mean, I know how Mormons use it, but it seems like it might have a different usage here." This was true for basic religious concepts such as baptism (remember Mallory's member check that reminded me that baptism does not carry the same connotation of a literal washing away of sin for evangelical Christians as it does for Mormons), but there were other terms that the participants used easily with each other that carried different meanings for me: *being convicted*, for example, is a term that I had never used as a religious person but that the participants used to describe the experience of realizing something about yourself that needs to change in order to be in God's will. During the last focus group, their shared language allowed them to ask each other questions and frame their arguments in ways that I wouldn't have or would have been previously unintelligible to me.

In these group portraits, the multiplicity and complexity of religious and teacher identities become clearer, as the teachers are in community with fellow Christian teachers who are working through some of the same moments of hesitation in varied ways. Equally, these portraits also stand as a reminder that the definition of an evangelical Christian is broad. Although all the participants would describe themselves as evangelical Christians, there is still a great deal of diversity in the religiously informed understandings they have of themselves, their students, and their purpose in the classroom.

The final chapter is also a group portrait in a broad sense in that it is the chapter where I offer my analysis of the data, where I blend my voice and bring my own theoretical and practical understandings to bear on the participants' experiences and words. It is a group portrait that includes and attempts to reveal the portraitist's stance and process, but it also serves as a reminder to readers that I am always and forever photobombing the portraits of the participants by inserting my own interpretations and analysis of their experiences and utterances. The first part of this chapter is my interpretation and analysis of the data and the portraits. I include in this portion some of the practical takeaways for teacher education and teacher induction programs, professional development planning, and future research. I also examine the limitations and affordances of the study. I then turn to an examination of my own ethics and moments of hesitation as a researcher and a portraitist. I explore the moments where the limits of my own hospitality were tested, where I made choices about what to filter, choose, and exclude in the portraits of the participants.

CHAPTER SEVEN

Portraits of Focus Groups

OUR FOCUS GROUPS MEET in a coffee shop that is about halfway between Noelle's and Mei's respective schools. This particular coffee shop was Mallory's idea—it's in the downtown area of the suburb she grew up in, and she tells me that there are tables in the back that are perfect for a focus group. She knows, she says with her self-deprecating smile, because she used to meet her mentors and her mentees here for Bible study. Our first focus group takes place in early December, so the lampposts lining the picturesque downtown shopping area are covered in holiday decorations—bells, snowflakes, candy canes, and holly. Twinkling lights cover storefronts, and as we walk into the coffee shop, a chalkboard sign announces in festive red and green that there will be free pictures with Santa. We tuck ourselves in at the back of the coffee shop after we get our coffees (hot chocolate for me, what with my aversion to the sinful smell of coffee), and we begin to get to know each other.

I think I'm the glue that holds everyone together here because Mallory, Mei, and Noelle are all from different cohorts of the same university program, but it turns out I'm wrong. Noelle immediately identifies Mallory as the roommate of her small-group leader from a campus religious organization and says, "I've been to your apartment!" After a few minutes of talk about their shared university experiences as English education majors, Mei realizes that she knows Mallory, too. Didn't they have a class together? Wasn't Mallory the person who stood up for her when the professor was picking on her about her religious beliefs? Wasn't that professor the worst?

Talking Theory Together

After the pleasantries and initial discussion, I turn on the recorder and pass out my handouts on Derridean ethics—the springboard I'll use to frame what a moment of hesitation looks like and that I hope they'll put up near their desk in their classroom to remind them of the kind of ethical decisions I'm most interested in studying. As I talk through the first section—the section on the aporia of (in)decision, I say, "I think it's possible to do a really Christian read of this. So if you have any comments you want to make or things you want to talk about, feel free to just interrupt me." They don't, of course; our pattern of teacher and students has been well established at this point, so I end up having to ask for their input. I say,

> Derrida sees that the impossibility of a decision having followed an ethical code is what requires us to actually make ethical choices. So every choice has to kind of take into account the context, has to take into account the responsibilities of that moment has to take into account the unique interpretations in that very moment. . . . Derrida is very much more interested in these really complicated situations where it feels impossible to make the same choice each time.

I pause, but no one steps into the beat, so I prompt, "Any thoughts on that one so far?"

Mei says flatly, "I think that's all teaching."

"Right," I say, agreeing. Mei continues by connecting what I've said to a classroom situation: she teaches several 21-year-old English-language learners who really need a diploma to be successful. But they are failing:

> There's so many different factors affecting every single student explaining why every single one of them is failing my class right now. . . . So—just—it does feel that it isn't possible for me to apply any sort of rule or legality to these decisions because it's the Christian in me that wants to do the thing that's what I think is perceived as best for them . . . and give them this diploma [even if they don't have the skills required to get it] . . . but then if I do it for one student, I have to do it for all these other students too, don't I?"

Mei has moved us effortlessly to the second section of our handout, so I jump in:

> So this is the second aporia we're talking about here . . . which is there's this tension between do I take care of the one person that's in front of me? Or do I also have a responsibility to everyone else, right? So Derrida says if I make a decision to feed my cat I have to be aware that there are millions of other starving cats around the world that I am *not* feeding. So these are the choices we make.

Mallory jumps in when I pause:

> It's like if I know a kid's religion and I know how they're perceiving something and I go out of my way to make sure they don't feel like othered or left out then I inevitably [other or leave out] the other people in the room or vice versa.

Noelle nods too and adds,

> I thought that too because I teach religions now because I teach social studies and language arts, and I take a lot of time to say, like, to word things very carefully about some of the religions. I know which ones my kids identify with and the ones they have experiences with, and I know that for the other religions [that students don't have experiences with], I'm not [being as careful with my words].

Noelle, as she often does, attends here to her sense that careful language usage can help to mask or neutralize some of the religious-political-social commitments of her (and her students') personal religious beliefs.

Mallory says thoughtfully, "It's tricky," and Noelle agrees: "It *is* tricky."

"So all of you have felt that tension certainly of wanting to attend to this child in front of you," I say.

> But you're also aware that if you attend to that you will be sacrificing something else . . . so that's part of what Derridean ethics is: that we make choices that can be seen as violent because we always exclude someone by including someone else or we cannot always make a decision with the full context.

"Violent?" Mei breaks in, "Like?" Her voice turns upward, inviting me to explain further.

"He uses violence in a broad sense," I say,

> like we cannot always care for others and ourselves perfectly. . . . But we have to make choices, because to do nothing is a form of violence for Derrida. So if we choose not to attend to poverty as a nation, that is also a form of violence because we could make different choices and we choose not to.

Noelle, Mei, and Mallory nod, and I get to the crux of how I want them to use Derridean ethics to define moments of hesitation for the study:

> And so what I'm really talking about is how do you as Christian teachers experience these moments where you have an understanding or a reckoning of who and what you're sacrificing when you make choices. What is informing your sense of it being an undecidable choice? What do you do in that moment?

Mei works to tie my Derridean framework into her Christian worldview: "Even if what we do is again, like singular . . . so the different factors that would lead to that one singular decision . . . is like, why that outcome came for this person or for this situation?" I nod, and she speaks more slowly. "Because the same factors are feeding into the choices, because if we believe that God is unchanging and his law is just—and if that's what's informed our decision. But you're saying that every single choice is like . . ." She trails off a little bit and then picks her train of thought back up again. "And then, so why is it if supposedly our source for decision making is the same to every decision, why is it that for this student I decide to let them fail. And for this student, I help them pass." She looks at me to make sure she's gotten the gist of my inquiry. Through her stumbling stops and starts, I wonder if Mei is trying to figure out if what I'm inquiring about is if Christian teachers are hypocrites. Possibly, too, she's pushing against my earlier assertion that it's possible to do a Christian reading of Derridean ethics, with Derrida's emphasis on undecidable contextualized decisions that might be different in every case. Here, she's asserting God's unchanging laws, asserting that she *wants* to make choices that are informed by an ethical code and that what's open for examination are the ways in which she, as a human, falls short of living up to her biblically informed ethics.

I try to clarify for her:

> Right. So I'm more thinking about what you do in those moments of hesitation and what part of your identity are you drawing from for those different choices and why. Like there might be places where you are aware that as a teacher you feel like you should make one choice but as a Christian you might want to make a different choice.

Mei pulls a face of exaggerated shock. "Oh, my God. There is a lot." Mallory and Noelle join in the laughter that acknowledges, yes, there is a lot to talk about.

Just like that, we start to think about how decisions get made in moments of hesitation. Mallory talks about how her current unit, *The Crucible*, (Miller, 1953) brings back memories of her own religious private high school experience with the play and how she's purposefully making different curricular choices in how she teaches the play. When she read it as a student, she remembers that "a lot of things fell down on Abigail" and that her teacher made a point of stopping the class to say, "Girls, this is what happens when you have sex before marriage, this is the result." She's chosen a different reading of the text as she works through it as a teacher in her own classroom, one in which Abigail's sexuality is a moment of power for her, a way to claim something of her own and to wield power in a space where she doesn't have much power because she's a woman. This is not to say that there's not a certain amount of anxiety when she says something that goes so blatantly against the sex-shaming purity culture she grew up in. She points out that she always feels a certain amount of angst when she makes these choices as a teacher because it feels so personally rebellious.

Mei talks about how she feels when the students she knows are Christian call her out for teacher behavior that they view as problematic or against God's plan for Christian women—specifically when she told her students she didn't want to get married:

> They basically said I shouldn't be so against it or I shouldn't close that door. And I can't tell them that I've chosen singleness as a path that God blesses upon people. Well, I probably should have said that, but I just moved on.

She reflects that it would be easier if she could just fix some of her Christian students' theological misunderstandings in that moment instead of hoping and trusting that God will fix those misunderstandings down the line.

Noelle talks about how she feels like she should let some of her students' parents know they failed the quiz on Christianity—especially students whose parents are ministers or heavily involved in Christian churches. "Like, of course, I failed as a teacher," she says, "and then also, on a more deep level: salvation." Her droll and matter-of-fact assessment of the situation is met with laughter and everyone begins to riff possible reactions for her. Mei starts, saying, "You're like: on the down low your child does not know this about Jesus." Mallory arranges her face in a prim, knowing, sly pout and mimes passing a paper to a child. "Have your parents sign this and bring this back." We laugh again and discuss Noelle's choices and responsibility in that moment as a teacher and as a Christian. To be clear, this exchange was meant as a joke and was understood by all of us as a joke, since all the teachers agreed that such behavior would be crossing a professional line in several ways. First, they would be holding their Christian students to a higher academic standard and would be involving parents in an issue that they normally wouldn't. Second, they felt that informing Christian parents about their children's religious beliefs with an intent to strengthen that belief was a clear overstep of the separation of church and state in public schools. But this joke is a telling moment of hesitation because the joke is literally that they feel a pull to make a different choice than the one Noelle made (which was to ultimately treat the quiz like any other quiz) because of their religious identities.

Undoubtedly because it's the end of the semester and grades are almost due, the conversation shifts to a discussion of assessment and the tension they feel in what it means to assess students fairly. Should they be honest? Should they give grace even when it feels dishonest to do so? Is it just to give grace to one student but not another? What do they do when their personal beliefs about grace and assessment run afoul of district or school policies?

At the end of the evening, we've been twice interrupted by store employees who just want to remind us that we can get our pictures taken with

Santa. Aside from the interruptions, our conversation has been wide-ranging and fruitful. I close the focus group by saying, "I genuinely did not think that assessment would be an issue, but I'm super excited by that, too. I mean, I expected we would talk about what happens when LGBTQ+ issues come up in your classrooms." Mei says, "I have some of that too." I wonder if they just weren't comfortable enough to talk to each other (and to me) about it yet. We gather our empty cups and head for the exit, walking back out onto the street that looks like a set for a Hallmark Christmas movie as we agree it was nice to see each other, it's been fun, and we'll see each other again soon.

Talking About LGBTQ+ Issues Together

During our second focus group, we meet at the same coffee shop and occupy the same table near the back. It's late February, which means it's bitterly cold for all the southerners and briskly chilly for everyone else. This time as I enter, I pass a middle-aged man in earnest conversation with a young adult man, both of them with their Bibles open in front of them. "What Samson teaches us here about sin is . . ." I'm past them before I can hear what Samson teaches us, but I give a half-smile. Mallory wasn't kidding when she said this was a hotspot for Bible studies. We go through all of our prerecording rituals: We grab our hot beverages and cup our hands around them for warmth as we exchange pleasantries. I fumble with the recorders and make my obligatory self-deprecating jokes about not being able to work technology.

Later, in a private conversation, Mallory shrewdly observes that I say, "Hang on, let me figure out how to work this!" every time I work technology—even while I do, clearly, know how to work it. I shrug, unoffended. "I know," I respond. "I do it to make myself nonthreatening. You do it too." She nods in agreement, equally unoffended. "I know I do; that's why I think it's funny."

After I turn on the recorder, our conversation about Derridean ethics and moments of hesitation begins in earnest. I idly wonder what passersby might think of our conversation, especially the Bible study crowd. My goal is to have the group talk about the larger themes that I saw in the moments of hesitation they shared with me in individual interviews and in their reflections: assessment, classroom management, student interactions, and welcoming LGBTQ+ students into their classrooms.

However, getting Noelle, Mallory, and Mei to talk about LGBTQ+ issues together in a focus group is like watching a ballet in which the dancers keep peeling away from the center of the stage before they ever arrive. I think we're getting close at several points in the conversation, but the conversation keeps veering away from the topic whenever we get too close. Mallory talks about "those who have been hurt by the church," and Mei talks about how she feels like people make assumptions about Christians and their ability to accept others and be kind. We're still dancing around the topic as Mallory talks about what moving away from a Christian perspective makes possible for her when she sees kids who have been hurt by people who are working from a Christian-informed worldview:

> Because we are in the South, if you identify as super not being a Christian, normally, you have a thing. Normally, there's *something* [that's hurt you within the Christian Church] and you have an assumption [that the church is hurtful] . . . and I don't want to claim any of those assumptions in my relationships with those kids.

I note the vague placeholder of "a thing" or "*something*" and consider that in our personal interviews, these placeholders didn't really exist.

Mei asks if those students "with strong hurt" might find healing if Mallory can embody being a good Christian teacher for those students. "Have you ever thought about possibly diving down deep, healing some of that or changing some of those assumptions [that those hurt kids might have about Christianity]?"

Mallory leans forward, gently clasps her hands together on the table, and speaks with conviction:

> I think I can heal those things without having anything to do with Christianity. I just think some of those things that are healed are healed through acceptance and love and kindness—the things that my upbringing gave me—but I don't always think that they're healed through them coming through Christ.

Mallory explains that she learned to be kind and learned to love others and learned selflessness ("but not necessarily acceptance") through her religious beliefs, but she says, "I think all of those are skills . . . they are just skills. They didn't go away [because I stopped being as religious]." Mei looks skeptical, her lips pursed as she thinks about how she might respond.

I finally break in because my patience with the careful dance and vague placeholders is wearing thin. "I mean, let's get specific. Are we talking about LGBTQ+ kids?"

Even then, Mallory seems hesitant. "Yeah, well . . ."

I press further but with more wiggle room. "Is that a good example?"

Mallory nods quickly, and finally (*finally!*), we start a direct conversation about the topic that has been pervasive in nearly every individual interview:

> That's a great example. . . . It's not just LGBTQ kids, but I do think that's a really easy one to look at, for sure. So, I look at that and those kids probably have felt hurt [by the overwhelming discourse of Christianity in the South] and I feel like I could heal that just as easily—if not more easily—without a Christian identity.

Mei frowns. It always seems to make her uneasy when she hears criticism of Christianity and Christian identities. "What is it that you're trying to heal?" she asks, a little defensively, "Their perceptions of Christians or their perceptions of themselves?" Here, we get to the crux of the argument that springs up between Mei and Mallory in this conversation. Mei's preferred choice is to change and improve the perceptions students might have about *Christianity*, which is why she wants to stand up for LGBTQ+ kids if they are being bullied. She doesn't want students to think that Christians are mean or unkind because they might not want to become Christians if they perceive Christianity in that way. It's why she wants to teach the Christians in her classroom that "they can't have that way of thinking or interacting with LGBT people" even when they do bring negative, religiously informed comments about LGBTQ+ identities into her classroom. If she can get the LGBTQ+ kids to understand that Christians don't see themselves as acting or speaking out of hate (even when it is hard for someone outside of the Christian discourse to frame their words and actions as anything but hate) and the Christian kids to understand how to effectively evangelize to LGBTQ+ students (by being nice to them while still insisting they are choosing to sin), she will have achieved her goals as a Christian teacher in a meaningful and substantive way. Her ultimate goal, then, is to heal students' perception of Christianity so that more people will want to be Christians. As it almost always is with Mei, she theoretically chooses evangelism as the most important demand of the situation.

Mallory's goal is different. When Mei asks her what she's trying to heal, she quickly responds, "Their perceptions of themselves." Yes, it's great, she says, if the way that she teaches empathy toward every person in a classroom—including Christian students—helps them to think through "putting yourself in other people's shoes and giving the other side the benefits of the doubt." If that exercise in empathy heals their perceptions of Christianity, fine. But it's not her primary goal. Her primary goal is to *be* accepting of LGBTQ+ kids' identities so that they know they matter. She talks through the tension she feels around the traditional view of Christian love she was raised with. There are times, she says, when if she *loves* someone in the Christian way, they will leave feeling corrected. No, she amends herself, "not even corrected: rejected. Because correction is different and it depends on the topic. But if we're talking about LGBTQ+ identities, I don't think there's a way to 'correct' without rejecting."

Mei can't or won't agree, of course, because her version of Christian love requires her to correct *and* reject, and both correction and rejection fall under the umbrella of love. As we're talking, I can see Mallory's irritation steadily building when confronted by Mei and her beliefs around kids and teachers and classrooms. Mei reveals another moment of hesitation that her complex (and uneven) interactions with students around LGBTQ+ issues and identities have brought about:

> I think it benefits my already-Christian-identifying students to see a religious person, who would traditionally be against LGBT people behaving in a way that is not—I don't want to say respectful, because I don't know if people think I'm respectful towards LGBT people, but at least, hopefully not as disrespectful as normal Christians are. The problem with that is, like today, through some weird misunderstanding, one of my class peers thinks I'm bi[sexual] and I don't know how to fix that.

Mallory takes a moment to neatly fold her hands between her legs and lean even farther across the table before she says in the hard, glittering tone that indicates that she is well and truly angry now, "Why did you feel like you have to fix it?"

Mei says, "Well, because I'm not bi[sexual] or even if I'm bi[sexual], I don't want them to think that I've embraced the bisexual lifestyle as a Christian."

Mallory feigns ignorance and curiosity, but I can see her laying a verbal trap to make her point. "But how is that different from you taking it as an insult?"

"Well, that's the thing. I don't want them to use that as an insult, but in my mind, I do view it as—"

"It insulted you, right?"

"It did not insult me."

"But for you, it's a sin." Mallory speaks decisively because she already knows Mei's answer.

But Mei doesn't falter. "Yes. What worried me is I don't want them to think you can be bisexual and a Christian at the same time."

Noelle says, "I have the same thing, actually. It's not like I'm offended; I'm concerned about their conception of what it means to be a Christian."

Mei nods gratefully at Noelle. "I think that's that main issue: I don't want that perception—the perception that it's okay to be bisexual and say, 'God is okay with it.'"

Noelle talks about how close she is with many of her students who do have LGBTQ+ identities (I'm sure she's thinking about Hannah), and she says that having such close relationships, through which the students know that she loves them, leave her "a little bit worried." She's worked hard for her students to be able to know that she really loves them "no matter who [they] are," but she also wants them to know that she does "not endorse a gay lifestyle as something that should be acted upon because I think that's a sin."

"Do you feel pressure to clarify that with other things that you think are sins?" Mallory asks. Noelle agrees that she doesn't, but this is an issue she's just more aware of, perhaps, because of the tension between her religious and teacher identity.

"It seems to me that you don't want it to be a bait and switch, right? Like, you're getting close with these kids. Is that true? The idea of 'I'm getting close to them. I'm showing them this love. We're starting to form a really good relationship.' If they find this out . . ." Mallory is pushing more gently now, perhaps because Noelle is less dogmatic than Mei.

Noelle breaks in. "Yeah, but it's like, most of them already know [I'm a Christian]. I wonder how they probably think—how they perceive my Christianity along with the fact that I accept you and will view you as a person. I don't know."

This conversation leads to several important takeaways about how the evangelical teachers in this study think about their interactions with and responsibilities to LGBTQ+ students. First, all the teachers viewed themselves as being more accepting of LGBTQ+ students than the average Christian. For Mallory, this is a source of pride, as she proudly states that she is "gay-affirming." For Mei and Noelle, this view of themselves is more nuanced; they are both proud of and ashamed of these moments when they might be more accepting than the average Christian. Mei calls herself, if not respectful of the LGBTQ+ community, at least "not as disrespectful as normal Christians are" setting herself apart from "normal" Christians who are, one assumes from the context, actively persecuting the LGBTQ+ community. Noelle's close relationships with LGBTQ+ students are something she's proud of. But for Mei and Noelle, this is simultaneously a source of anxiety. Being accepting of LGBTQ+ identities is positioned again and again by both Mei and Noelle as antithetical to their evangelical beliefs. Mei wants students to be clear that she would never "embrace the bisexual lifestyle as a Christian." Surprisingly, Noelle, who tends to mask so much of her personal belief with careful language choice, is crystal clear on the same point: She worries her acceptance of students with LGBTQ+ identities gives students the wrong perception of her Christianity. For Mei and Noelle, the moments when they accept and offer hospitality to their LGBTQ+ students might be ethically defensible from a professional perspective and maybe even in line with their Christian call to love everyone unconditionally, but they do not see them as moments when they are behaving in a "normal" Christian way or standing up for their Christian values. Noelle can't be more explicit than when she says that the fact that her students know she is a Christian is hard because they might not be able to reconcile "my Christianity along with the fact that I accept [them] and will view [them] as a person."

I hesitate to put too much emphasis on a single phrase because I am aware that all of us misspeak or say things that are linguistically imprecise as we attempt to express ourselves. However, in this statement, Noelle (and Mei makes similar rhetorical moves) sets her Christianity at odds with her willingness to accept LGBTQ+ students each *as a person*. She worries that her willingness to form meaningful relationships with LGBTQ+ students isn't an evolved form of Christianity with a broadening definition of unconditional love but is instead completely incompatible with Christianity. This conflict speaks directly to the question of how religious, evangelical Christian teachers are determining who is a stranger who deserves hospitality and who is "the being that is not" (Derrida, 1997/2000, p. 5). Remember that offering hospitality to a stranger has an effect on the host as well, as strangers question and disturb the ways of thinking and doing and being that the host has already established. All three of the teachers in this study experienced the disorientation of having their comfortable, religiously informed ways of thinking challenged by the arrival of a student/stranger whose identity demands a recalibration of what it means to welcome unconditionally, to love unconditionally. Although all the participants viewed themselves as offering some kind of hospitality to LGBTQ+ students, the rhetorical moves by Noelle and Mei indicate a certain amount of religiously informed apprehension in including LGBTQ+ students in their determination of the kind of stranger who is worthy of hospitality. In such instances, Noelle and Mei identify LGBTQ+ students as "beings that are not."

The blithe, bright violence to the other is the point here, discursively at least. When violence is an essential characteristic of love—especially the definition of religious "unconditional" love that participants are working to embody in their classrooms—the exclusions of LGBTQ+ students become more than just commonsensical. That violence and exclusion take on a spiritual, religious, and godly quality. The inclusion of LGBTQ+ students, by contrast, is personally and religiously uncomfortable for both Noelle and Mei because inclusion does not hold the violence necessary to show Christian love. This aporia of unconditional love being predicated on exclusion—an aporia that is so clear to outside observers—is an aporia that participants themselves wrestle with. While in LGBTQ+-affirming spaces, there is a commonsensical argument that it is impossible to love or accept or care for those with LGBTQ+ identities while rejecting their sexual and gender identities. The participants here see that aporia too, but their conclusions (with the exception of Mallory, of course) are different. Because of their religiously informed conceptions of love, it is impossible for them to love or accept or care for those with LGBTQ+ identities *without* making clear their rejection of that identity.

The second important takeaway is the participants' understanding that teaching offers the opportunity to show forth God's love (even Mei, who is often frustrated by policies and procedures as she works to evangelize, understands teaching as an evangelical opportunity to show God's love). Orienting classroom practice to their own religious identity allows participants to carry their personal interpretations of how God's love is defined and how God's love is enacted when confronted with otherness. This was evident in the individual portraits, but it is certainly worth amplifying here: When the participants talk about how they are trying to *unconditionally* love their students, that love actually comes with plenty of conditions (remember the message of love throughout Mallory's childhood: "I love you too much to let you be the way you are"). These conditions on love are what make space for uneven enactments of hospitality: Forgiveness might be offered to one student but not another in classroom management situations; the "love" given to LGBTQ+ students might be an evangelical maneuver or accompany deep personal uneasiness about the student's identity.

Third, this conversation illuminates the enthusiasm evangelical Christian teachers have for time and space to engage in theoretical, pedagogical, and religious discussions with each other as they work to make sense of their experiences as evangelical Christians and teachers. Particularly in this final focus group, my role as an interviewer was much easier: All the participants had their own questions for each other and worked to tease out the doctrines that accounted for their differences in beliefs about teaching, classrooms, and kids. At one point, Noelle and Mallory asked a rapid-fire series of questions to Mei to try to tease out why they believed teaching was compatible with their beliefs as an evangelical Christian (and even described it as a "sanctifying experience") when she didn't. As they talked through various Christian concepts like grace, election, and perfection, Mei identified that the difference is that she doesn't view God's ultimate goal as loving his children but rather as producing glory through the salvation or damnation of his children—both of which equally serve to show forth God's glory. This kind of religio-professional talk was highly valued by the participants, who admitted that they never felt they could or should have these conversations with fellow teachers at their schools.

Final Touches: Unpacking the Study

I ask Mei, Mallory, and Noelle to reflect on what the benefits and drawbacks of participating in this study have been for them. There's a thoughtful silence before Mei responds:

> I think the benefit is just . . . reflecting, and remembering a lot of my old priorities that might have mellowed out through teaching. The spiritual priorities that I [have] shouldn't have mellowed out but [they] did. It helped me realize a lot of like why, I'm struggling spiritually right now. . . . I've grown in experience for teaching but I've really fallen away in terms of my relationship with God. It's made me a little bit—it's nice because I understand a little bit of why I'm having a weird, I mean, a weird funk right now, spiritually. But it's also sad because I'm thinking like, "Where do I go from here?" It's beneficial, but it's also a little deflating.

Mei cups her coffee cup with both hands as she looks down. She's sharing a vulnerable moment with the group, but it's hard to admit how hard teaching as a profession has been for her.

Mallory builds her response off Mei's, acknowledging Mei's point and reflecting her tendency to build consensus whenever possible:

> I think, similarly, the thing I've really appreciate[d] from it is the reflection time . . . once you get into teaching . . . you just don't have any time to sit and reflect . . . you don't take the time a lot of times to think about your choices and how you make the choices you're making. So, having that forced time to think through the ethics of my choices and why I made them, I think was probably the most beneficial part for me.

When Mei wonders if it's more that teachers just take time to reflect on lessons and the teaching moves they make, Mallory clarifies:

> Yeah, automatically you reflect on how lessons went, right? That's something that's always happening because I'm like, "Well, maybe I should change that." But because you're not going to repeat an interaction with a

> kid and you're not going to repeat a relational moment, I think that takes more time to sit and think about. Because if you do a lesson in first period, of course, you're going to reflect on what you might change for second or third. But when a thing happens with a kid, an ethical moment or a moment with how you choose to react or whatever, that is where you don't always sit—or I don't always sit—and reflect on like, "Hey, if that would ever happen again, what would be the ethics that I walk into it with?" So, that's been helpful.

Noelle agrees. She says that what she's appreciated the most as a participant in the study is thinking through the process of why she makes decisions. She says that she has a sense that some of her decision-making processes are invisible to her—not that they are "robotlike," but the thought process behind the decision-making is "so engrained in the way I would normally make decisions." She says it's been a nice reminder that she does have reasons behind doing what she does.

Mallory asks if Noelle is thinking about if those reasons are the reasons she wants them to be, and Noelle nods. "Most of the time it has been, but if it's not, I'm like, 'Oh, I should address that.'" The consensus, in general, is that being reflective about the decision-making process for those moments of hesitation has made space for them to examine the alignment of their classroom practice with their beliefs and theoretical stances. For Mei, that's meant examining how her religious identity has suffered; for Mallory, that's meant examining the ethical stances she takes in relational moments; for Noelle, it's meant that she thinks about whether she's making decisions purposefully, with the intent she wants to make them with.

When I return to asking them about drawbacks, only Mallory responds. She says, "I felt overwhelmed in some ways—especially when we've talked about the idea of everything being a violence." Here, Mei nods in agreement but stays silent as Mallory keeps talking:

> It's easier when I don't think through how I'm always picking someone [to privilege]. Sometimes it's me and sometimes it's a kid and sometimes it's the majority of the kids. . . . I think it's been helpful, but it is disheartening.

I try a different approach to draw Noelle and Mei into the conversation as well:

> As we've talked in our one-on-one interviews, all of us have talked about these moments of hesitation. What it is about those moments of hesitation that make them so uncomfortable or so difficult to navigate? Why are they moments of hesitation?

Noelle raises one hand a few inches off the table to indicate that she'll talk first:

> Those are moments where it's very, like, you can't avoid knowing that you can make a mistake. Sometimes you don't have to always think about that, but when I have one of those moments, I can't not think, "I can make a mistake here."

Mallory is quick to affirm this reading of a moment of hesitation. She says,

> Yeah, there's an alarm that goes off in my head that's like, "This matters. This next step is going to matter to someone," and it takes you out of the automated part of teaching where you're just going and doing your thing.

Noelle echoes the language of the aporia of urgency when she adds, "Yeah, I've got to make a decision, and it has to be now." Noelle and Mallory, both of whom feel a lot of religiously informed pressure to be perfect, to make the *right* decision, to ascertain God's will and stay in it, share a sense that moments of hesitation occur because there might be a mistake or because the choice is too important to get wrong.

Noelle and Mallory both sense that moments of hesitation are worth talking about because they are moments that *matter to someone*. This sense that these ethically difficult moments *matter* because they are interactions with the Derridean other reflects their understanding of classrooms as places where students are grappling with more important and complex matters than just dry content—where to place a comma, for example, or the correct usage of a particularly meaty vocabulary word. Instead, they view classrooms as places where students learn as much from the personal interactions between teacher and student and the discourse of the classroom and the school as they do from more standardized curriculum elements. It also reflects their understanding of their role as teacher as a role that *matters* and requires far more complex calibrations of interaction, care, and responsibility than may be accounted for in the larger discourse about what constitutes good teaching. Edgoose (2001) points out that these moments are not only moments of hesitation but often moments of discomfort as well, when educators "are exposed with an important ethical sensitivity." The participants' experiences and reports of the discomfort of these moments indicate that they were aware of their own exposure to ethics and responsibility. A study of these moments of hesitation, with the participants in this study and throughout this book, is most valuable because it exposes the ethical vulnerability inherent in the act of teaching. The path to justice in a classroom is made up of fragmented, ethically difficult interactions with students that may be impossible to fully understand, Edgoose says, but the "loss of understanding and fluency" that comes with these ethical aporias is a key component to navigating moments that *matter to someone* ethically. Certainly, the shared discussions between participants in this study attest to the difficulty—and value—of sitting in those moments of discomfort and hesitation, of recalibrating their response to the demands of their personal, religious, and professional identities.

References

Derrida, J. (2000) *Of hospitality: Anne Dufourmantelle invites Jacques Derrida to respond* (R. Bowlby, Trans.). Stanford University Press. (Original work published 1997)

Edgoose, J. (2001). Just decide! Derrida and the ethical aporias of education. In G. J. Biesta & D. Egea-Kuehne (Eds.), *Derrida & education* (pp. 119–133). Routledge.

Miller, A. (1953). *The crucible*. Penguin Books.

CHAPTER EIGHT

Photobombing the Portraits: Analyzing the Portraits and the (In)Hospitality of Research

When I talk about this research with other teacher educators, first, almost always they express a hesitation of their own in the way they interact with religious identities in their own teacher training programs, but second, the question is always, "So what should we *do* with them? Do we counsel them out of the profession? Is there a way to change their minds about social justice education?" These questions reflect some of the assumptions that liberal university educators might have about religious identities, but it is also a reflection of the personal experiences that some educators have had with some religious preservice teachers—a reflection of a general anxiety that perhaps religious teachers (particularly those who identify as evangelical Christian) might not be going into teaching to enact the same version of social change that teacher educators have prioritized.

A clear and universal answer to this question of what we might *do* with evangelical Christian teachers is beyond the scope of this research, but this research does complicate the idea that there might be a single best answer. What these complicating portraits suggest is that teacher training and teacher induction approaches should be highly contextualized and consider individual dispositions for equity. Of these three teachers, all three identify themselves as attending to diversity, teaching for social justice and equality (especially when defined in terms of race and ethnicity—Mei and Noelle are less attentive to gender and sexual difference), but they equally see their teaching as a form of evangelism and a project of conversion. Although there is a broader pattern here of education as evangelism, there is also a great deal of individual difference in the practice of each teacher, as each teacher picks up and enacts religious conceptions that frame their teacher identity and practice in different ways.

There were several themes that carried through multiple participants' portraits (including the group portrait) and are worth noting here. Teacher practice for multiple participants was influenced by Christian conceptions of confession, repentance, and forgiveness and God's love and sovereignty.

Confession, Forgiveness, and Repentance

Both Mallory and Noelle made decisions about the way they interacted with students based on Christian ideals of confession, repentance, and forgiveness. Mallory's decision to write a letter of support for a student who has sexually assaulted a girl is heavily influenced by the student's confession of wrongdoing and expression of guilt and remorse. Noelle, on the other hand, identifies herself as "offering grace" to students who have forgotten their homework if they seem to be upset and contrite. For Mei, confession, repentance, and forgiveness are equally important to her sense of classroom practice, but she is also preoccupied with the way that the repeated demands of her job make *her own* repentance process impossible. Because she knows her fear of losing her job will cause her to continue to let opportunities to evangelize students pass by, she cannot fully repent because she cannot perform the change that true repentance requires of her.

What both of these approaches to repentance and forgiveness indicate, regardless of whether the participants have an interior (Mei) or an exterior (Mallory and Noelle) orientation toward it, is the importance of confession as a discursive disciplinary practice (Foucault, 1990) for the evangelical teachers in this study. Foucault's concept of confession is much broader than simply an act of admitting wrongdoing, it is, in fact, "a disclosure of the self; it is a discourse of identity rather than apology" (Tell, 2007, p. 1). Confession, repentance, and the forgiveness that it is tied to exist then as a way of identifying a subject who gets to be a subject. It might be a condition of hospitality, a way of distinguishing the being who is from the being who is not. As we consider what this makes possible for evangelical teachers in public classroom spaces, we might attend to what it means when evangelical teachers encounter students who can't or won't perform a version of confession and repentance that their evangelical teachers recognize as worthy of forgiveness. This discursive formation around confession and repentance might mean that evangelical teachers who have the goal of showing grace to students predicate that grace on a student's performance of Christianity.

God's Love and God's Sovereignty

Christian conceptions around God's love and God's sovereignty were equally important to all three participants and were often talked about as deeply influencing the way participants interacted with students. The goal as a teacher, for all three participants (although Mallory shifted between a present/past orientation toward this goal), was explicitly stated as "showing forth God's love." Individual conceptions of what God's love entailed determined how individuals positioned themselves in the classroom. For Mallory, showing forth God's love meant that students needed to feel loved, enjoyed, and accepted. For Noelle, showing forth God's love meant that students needed to see her as cheerful, patient, and kind. For Mei, showing forth God's love meant that students needed to be sacrificed for in terms of giving up her own money, giving her time by staying after school with struggling students, and giving up her lunches for students who were hungry. However, God's love had also been consistently defined in religious spaces as a call to change people, to call them to account, to "love [them] too much to let [them] be the way [they] are."

The conception around God's sovereignty matters for all the participants as well. For Mallory and Noelle, the idea that God's will is wide and he has the ability to turn all things for good meant that they were much more content to let moments of direct and explicit evangelism pass by. They believed that students would hear the Gospel in some other way and that their examples were sufficient. Mei's belief in God's sovereignty allows her to be very bold in her evangelism—to say things that others might take up as harsh or critical—with the knowledge that God could turn them to good.

All these conceptions of God's love and God's sovereignty make it possible for all three teachers to position themselves as hosts in their classrooms, to view themselves as one who offers hospitality (a concept that they seemed to loosely equate with the unconditional love of God in our focus group discussions) to the other or determines who is excluded from hospitality as a being who is not. The limits on this hospitality, because hospitality always contains limits, is bounded by each participant's individual understanding of what God's love is and entails and what God's sovereignty makes possible.

Implications of Research

These research portraits have implications for several areas of broader educational research, including research on teacher training and induction, research on the role of religion in public education, and English education.

What this research challenges within the fields of teacher training, teacher induction, and religion and education is an assumption that teachers can leave their religious identities at the schoolhouse door. Assumptions of religious neutrality help no one—it leaves teachers feeling as though they have to navigate their identity as a religious teacher on their own (Ahn et al., 2016) with very little guidance beyond "Just don't talk about it." And while there are evangelical Christians like Mei who are actively committed to verbally evangelizing in public classrooms, this research suggests that there is far more to the religious identities of teachers than what they *say* in classrooms. The evangelical Christians in this study tied their religious identity to their purpose for teaching, their concept of what it means to be a teacher, their concept of students, and the way they approached classroom discipline.

Mei's portrait, particularly her deep unhappiness with who she is becoming as a result of public school teaching, might open up new possibilities for important discussions within teacher education programs. I couldn't help but think how much it might have helped Mei to have a frank and open conversation with an advisor or an instructor who was honest about the ways in which Mei might find teaching to be an unsatisfactory profession as a Christian who is committed to evangelism everywhere and in everything. This kind of conversation, whereby a concern for Mei's personal fulfillment and spiritual health is the central focus, might have enabled Mei to make different decisions about the teaching profession based on her own "spiritual walk"—which Mei prioritizes over some of the other arguments teacher educators might make to dissuade her from teaching. It is impossible to know what Mei's response to that would have been, but her disillusionment with public school teaching suggests that she envisioned her performance of teacher as vastly different from what she feels able to perform within her classroom. More honest and frank conversations about what teaching with an evangelical Christian identity might and might not look like would, in my opinion, be helpful for evangelical preservice teachers.

While teacher training has often focused on practice-based skills (classroom management, instructional strategies, assessment strategies, etc.) and teacher induction has focused on providing expert mentors to extend this practical professional knowledge,[1] this research highlights the importance of engaging *all* teachers with theoretical approaches that might allow them to consider their own conceptions of educational hospitality and their own identities. In terms of professional development, this attention to theory may be more useful once teachers have a year or two of teaching completed, after they have figured out a workable approach to planning, classroom management, and teacher–student interactions. For first-year teacher Noelle, I sometimes felt that I was asking her to attend to moments of hesitation when all her teaching decisions had the quality of a moment of hesitation due to the often overwhelming demands of the first year of teaching.

More specifically, attending to theoretical approaches allows teachers to consider (as Derrida invites them to consider), if the current commitment to hospitality—with all its limits and exclusions—is the version of hospitality that education, broadly speaking, and individual teachers, more narrowly speaking, are committed to enacting in their own classrooms. Derrida (1997/2001) would likely agree that engaging with theory is important for teachers but on an even larger scale, because one of his more practical projects was advocating for the inclusion of a mandatory year of philosophy in French secondary schools,[2] a move that he felt would open discourses to new interpretations of the responsibility owed to other humans, particularly within his deconstruction of hospitality and cosmopolitanism. In short, Derrida believed that exposure and explorations within theory allowed for a deconstruction of the other, an improvement of the concept of the subject (Derrida, 2001), and a more nuanced and generous welcoming in of the other—certainly work worth doing in public school classrooms.

Particular to the field of English education, all three participants talked about how their choice to teach language arts over another topic was driven by their perception that language arts classrooms allowed them to talk about real issues, to interact more personally and build stronger relationships with students as they responded to and with literature. This is an important link because all the participants also viewed their role as a teacher to be tied to evangelism, whether it was a soft evangelism of showing a loving and caring example or a more direct evangelism of speaking out about their own faith. The very nature of language arts classrooms was most appealing to these participants *because* the content of language arts classrooms makes the kinds of relationships and discussions possible that effective evangelism requires. However, the moments of hesitation that most concerned the participants centered on their interactions with students and were not necessarily centered on content.

Additionally, the findings of this research might suggest one possible reason that teachers are resistant to challenging the overwhelming inclusion of canonical texts that center the White, Christian, Eurocentric way of being, even if they view themselves as educators who are working for equity, as the participants of this study did. Part of this, as participants reflected within this study, is the emphasis on authoritative texts within their religious tradition—a way of viewing literacy and reading that may cause them to choose books that have been imbued with a certain amount of authority within the larger cultural discourse. But what was more striking to me, particularly in Mallory's narrative, was that Mallory chooses to teach *The Great Gatsby* (Fitzgerald, 1925) because through her own reading of it with a religious identity, it has become a *sacred* text to her, and she wants her students to experience a similarly powerful literary experience, although she stops short of framing her students' reading the book in her classroom as an explicitly religious experience. She recounts, as a young teenager reading the story herself for the first time, writing journals tying the story's narrative to her spiritual understanding of the Bible and noting how she found God within the text. Although there are other places in the curriculum where she includes diverse texts—including an end-of-year book-club unit that encourages students to read young adult literature that attends to gender, sexual, racial, and ethnic diversity—she continues to position *The Great Gatsby* as a defining feature of her American literature course, largely because of her own reverence for the text.

Limitations and Affordances of This Study

I chose to use portraiture as the methodology of this study to attend to the goodness of these evangelical Christian participants (particularly according to their own definition of goodness) as they navigate their classroom spaces. This decision insisted that I attended not only to data collection and analysis but also to the representation of the data—particularly to how I might write my findings in a way that makes the data accessible to a public beyond fellow educational researchers. The use of portraiture also meant that I was more visible in the write-up of the research in ways that other methodologies and traditional research reports have often attempted to obscure. I consider these aspects of portraiture, which allow for a more complicated and complicating portrayal of evangelical Christian teachers, to be affordances of this study.

On the flip side of this, there were moments when my portraiture-centered stance toward my participants—a stance that committed me to a generous reading of their beliefs and practices and which I purposefully selected to keep me from sensationalizing or decontextualizing their responses—occasionally forced me to draw back and pull myself back from fully expressing my reaction to these beliefs and practices. Although I tried to balance my commitment to present the participants as members of a discourse whereby their beliefs and practices were commonsensical and logical with my commitment to consider how the participants' religious discourses might conflict or at least chafe against the larger educational discourse in which they worked, the portraitist's stance remains a point of concern for this study. It is enough, perhaps, to point out that my attempt to present a participant such as Mei as a product of a discourse that creates her stance toward LGBTQ+ youth, gender, masculinity, and feminism as reasonable within that discourse might have worked to erase from the presented portrait my own deep unease with such a discourse. While I did not wish to portray her as "crazy" or "ignorant," a different theoretical and methodological approach might have allowed me to more critically engage with some of her more problematic stances. As it is, I have left some of that work to readers themselves to interpret and evaluate, which is compatible with the aims of portraiture but which caused me a certain amount of anxiety about the way that both she and I would be interpreted and read as a result of these portraits.

Another affordance (or limitation, depending on perspective) of a portraiture study like this one is that multiple readings of the same portrait are possible. The reader is equally invited to make meaning of the portraits, to read the portrait as both a research report *and* a literary piece, to engage with the author's imagery, symbols, and word choice. There are pieces of the representations of these participants that seem contradictory, that stand in contrast to something they themselves said in a different situation, on a different page, in a different paragraph. One of the affordances of portraiture (and one that postconstructions of reading and literacy support) is a positioning of the reader as someone who has to *work* to make meaning. As such, I did not feel obligated to explain the significance of every single phrase. In fact, I have purposefully left some of these details and word choices stand alone to honor the ambiguity of interpretation that portraits and other aesthetic representations always, by nature, open to their audiences.

I attempted to attend to diversity in research sites and research participants for this study, and although there is only a limited amount of diversity that is possible within a small participant pool like this one, I found the variety of experiences and backgrounds (religiously and demographically) to be an affordance of this attention to difference within the participant pool. However, I did also limit certain variables, selecting participants who graduated from the same teacher preparation program and are teaching in the same school district. Although I did not theorize or purposefully select only teachers who identify as female, all the participants identify as women. A limitation of this study might be that the gendered experiences of the participants were not adequately attended to within the study itself. It is worth noting, however, that while I see strong discursive elements in the concept of teaching and teachers that are highly gendered (in the vein of Grumet, 1988, who examined the strong parallels between the discourses of motherhood and teacher), participants themselves often rejected this notion. They might refer in our interviews to what it meant to be a Christian woman and a teacher, but they never separated their concept of womanhood from their religious belief, nor did they ever attempt to examine their teaching as an exclusively gendered practice. None of the participants ever attributed their sense of care for students, for example, to a desire to be like a mother to their students; instead, that was universally attributed to their Christian beliefs about their own ability to show God's love.

Although I collected data from various sources—interviews, Flipgrid reflections, classroom artifacts, and focus groups—this study would have been much different if I had included observations of the teachers in their classroom settings and examined their interactions with students. Because it was not possible to obtain permission from the school district in which the participants teach to observe for an extended period, this study relied on the participants' self-awareness of their own moments of hesitation. In many ways, this particular limitation focused this study as an examination of teachers' own perceptions of their religious identities as evangelical Christians and moments of hesitation about these identities within their classrooms.

The Portraitist's Stance—Hospitable Research and Ethical Choices

A Derridean framework for this research opens opportunities for a reflection of the ways in which I, as a researcher, attempted to offer hospitality to the participants of the study and worked to make ethical choices about the study by considering responsibility, undecidability, and urgency. In a very broad sense, this study was my attempt, as a now-liberal, religiously skeptical teacher educator, to consider how I welcome in the other in my own research (and university teaching), how I position myself as a host who offers an unlimited welcome without ceding self or autonomy, and how I consider how I, as a researcher, might be limiting that welcome. Some of this, it should be pointed out, is also a grappling with my own past identities or an attempt to make sense of my own past performances of discursive, systemic, religiously informed acts of homophobia, transphobia, racism, and misogyny.

It would be fair to say that I experienced my own moments of hesitation as a researcher. The majority of my moments of hesitation mirrored my participants' moments of hesitation in that I was often considering how my own beliefs about education and the role of teachers were sometimes in conflict with the beliefs and practice of the participants. I spent a great deal of time considering what I might *do* with that discomfort as a researcher. I was committed to reading my participants generously—in fact, I had built my entire study around this guiding principle of hospitality and generosity. But there were certainly times when I found myself feeling less than generous and considering the limits of my own hospitality. I worried over the representation of these moments in the portraits. This was nowhere more obvious than with issues of gender and sexuality in classroom spaces, which I intend to unpack here.

I'm not interested, particularly, in presenting my process as the *right* process or in claiming expertise in researcher ethics that would function to conceal the actual difficulty of the research process. Instead, I wish to highlight here some of the choices I made, explaining why I made them within the theoretical framework I was using and how I navigated my own moments of hesitation. As Edgoose (2001, p. 132) points out, I expose my own ethical sensitivity and vulnerability by examining "the discontinuities . . . and aporetic punctuation of the codes of morality and knowledge" of my own research process.

One of the decisions I made very deliberately was the choice to engage and center the conversation of the participants on theory, in this case around Derrida's exploration of the aporias inherent in responsible decision-making. Although I made this decision initially to build a shared language around what a "moment of hesitation" might look like, and as a way of establishing a loose sense for the unit of measurement of the study, I found that engaging participants with theory actually ended up having implications for my stance as a hospitable researcher as well. Centering theory allowed participants to analyze and work through their own responses and encouraged me as a researcher to engage participants in analyzing their own experiences. As participants noted, the focus on theory in our interviews and focus groups made the study valuable to them—all the participants noted that participating in the study made space for them to examine the alignment of their personal beliefs with their classroom practices. If we had not discussed the underlying theory of the study and I had chosen instead to simply extract their stories without the theoretical mandate to discuss—with the participants themselves in the moment of the telling of the story—the commitments of those choices, the opportunity for self-examination would have been greatly minimized.

One of the ways in which I centered hospitality with my participants was in my stance as an interviewer and as a focus group mediator. I attempted (and it should be noted that I am a fairly relational person in general) to engage each participant as an empathetic and interested person. There were times with each participant where we shared genuine human emotion and connection. It was just as emotional for me to talk with Noelle about her breakup as it was to talk to Mei about the anguish she felt about her own spirituality as it was to talk about the truly undecidable character reference with Mallory. In the interviews, it felt quite easy to center myself in that moment,[3] with that participant, with these emotions—all with the understanding that I was committed to a conversation in which I "*speak* to you, I *address* you, I *listen* to you" (Derrida, 2001, p. 180). Like Mallory,

I found hospitality to be fairly easy to offer in individual settings and much more complicated when I considered how to be hospitable to multiple others simultaneously. What might it mean then to create a portrait that is hospitable to the subject itself but is also hospitable to readers who approach it from a different viewpoint? Have I done damage to LGBTQ+ youth by representing the homophobia and transphobia of some participants as *commonsensical* within their discourse? It is not my intention here to cause damage to *anyone* but instead to open conversations about how these discursive figurations might be opened up to new configurations. Derrida again would remind me that every choice is a violence to someone; is it enough to say that I weighed the violences and attempted to responsibly enact them?

When in doubt, I perhaps erred on the side of welcoming in the otherness of the participants in front of me. Mallory's response to being asked to write a character reference ultimately centered her responsibility to the student in front of her at that moment, and I found myself making similar choices in my representation of the participants (although they might argue otherwise, of course). In particular, I specifically chose *not* to describe Mei's beliefs and actions as homophobic within her portrait, although I think the term is an accurate description. Some of this was an attempt to portray Mei in a way that she would recognize herself (a key aim of portraiture) because she doesn't view herself as homophobic but as embodying God's love. However, I was also making a conscious effort to offer hospitality in a place and in a way in which it was hard for me to offer hospitality. Instead of centering my own reaction to Mei, I chose to represent her in a way that recognized her as the subject of her own experience; in short, I wanted readers to hear her story before telling my own. I also consciously retreated in these moments into a heavier reliance on the words of the participant themselves (as with the poetry portrait of Noelle's response to a transitioning student, which is entirely created from her own words) to portray who they were and what they were experiencing in those moments. This retreat was intentional, but it does open space for a critique in my own performance of hospitality, whereby I prefer to cede the responsibility of the portrait to the hosted instead of maintaining my sovereignty as the host.

Although I did send the portraits to the participants in an attempt to make sure that I was accurately reading and interpreting their words and our interviews, this does not mean that the participants were always pleased and delighted by the portraits that I created for them. Although I tried to create the portraits out of my deep affection and respect for religious teachers, there were places where my interpretation of the participants stung or felt too critical or too personal, for a variety of reasons. But there were other places where they reported the portrait invited them to reexamine their practice again (Mei, for example, responded to my interpretation of her saying "Oh, you two like to be close to each other?" to two male students as a sideways enforcement of gender norms by committing to rethink the ways in which she made assumptions about students). In the places in the portraits where participants reported feeling discomfort with my portrayal of them, I revisited those passages again to make sure that I was accurately representing my reading of participants' intentions and beliefs. Those places, like Mallory's undecidable character reference, were most marked by ethical complexity, vulnerability, and undecidability. While I tried to accurately convey my understanding of the discursive frameworks that participants were using to make decisions, my understandings and readings can (and should) be placed within my own discursive framework, which, of course, leaves my interpretations open to critique in other frameworks.

I remain committed to complex, complicating, and hospitable research in general. As a researcher who experienced the aporias inherent in performing hospitality *and* in making ethical decisions throughout this process, I still find that the possibility these impossibilities open up attends to important considerations of research ethics and responsibility. In my own performance of researcher hospitality, I am still grappling with how I might balance the demands of being a generous *and* critical researcher, especially in terms of the representation of research.

In Closing

Broadly, the purpose of this book was to examine how evangelical teachers' religious identities shape their performance of "teacher" in public school classrooms, particularly with an eye to how these religious identities informed the participants' ability and desire to welcome in the other or to offer hospitality. This book, then, while perhaps falling far short of providing a workable and practical solution for how we might "fix" or "reconcile" the aporia that religious teaching identities in public education systems present, is an attempt to plumb the aporia—to understand the exclusions; the commonsensicality that creates blithe, bright violence against the excluded; and the ways in which school and classroom communities are always built on closure and exclusion. Overwhelmingly, Christian-informed views of gender, sexuality, repentance, forgiveness, and sovereignty shaped participants' conceptions of hospitality and defined the conditions of possibility for hospitality in their classrooms, even when the participants themselves were cognizant of trying to enforce the separation of church and state that they understood as a necessary part of their teacher identity in a public school system.

What *is* clearest, then, from this study is that teachers' religious identities in public school systems have deep relevance to the current enactment of public education and to the future possibilities of educational change or reforms. Obviously, as an educational researcher, I would call for more complex and complicating research around religious teacher identity: research that attempts to account for, understand, examine, and loosen religious discursive figurations that limit hospitality within classrooms, especially to groups that are already often the least welcomed in societies. But as a teacher educator, I also call for teacher education and teacher induction that invite preservice and new teachers to engage with their religious identities not with the intent to annihilate those identities but with the intent of inviting self-reflection on all the ways—good, bad, and ugly—that religious identity informs classroom practice and teacher identity. Although I found engaging new teachers with Derridean ethics theoretical approaches helpful, there might be other, more efficacious approaches.

Part of "taking religion seriously," as Nord and Haynes (1998) urged, is to take very seriously the power that religious discourses, religious beliefs, and religious identities have had in shaping educational discourses—especially around the fundamental purpose of education. Taking religion seriously requires taking seriously how pervasively religious discourse and religious identity already exist in public school classrooms and shape a great deal of societal notions about what it means to be a good teacher or a good student. What taking religion seriously might also mean is making space for new performances of school community, teacher care, student responsibility, instruction, and assessment by making plain the way religious discourses have circumscribed past and current interpretations of these topics and many others. As Derrida would certainly point out, deconstruction and the laying bare of the commitments of discursive figurations are meant to invite a *re-construction* with an eye to an improvement or broadening of the concept of subject—a more inclusive concept of who gets to be a being that is.

Notes

1. I do not mean to argue that teachers do not need practical professional knowledge. I believe practical know-how to be is a vital and important part of learning to be a teacher. I suggest here simply that practical know-how that is theoretically unexamined might be insufficient.
2. This is the equivalent to high school in the United States.
3. This stance, it might be pointed out, dovetails nicely with the social skills I learned as a Mormon girl and woman, where the comfort of others is far more important than my own discomfort.

References

Ahn, J., Hinson, D. W., & Teets, S. T. (2016). Teachers' views on integrating faith into their professional lives: A cross-cultural glimpse. *AILACTE Journal, 13*(1), 41–57.

Derrida, J. (2001). Talking liberties: Jacques Derrida's interview with Alan Montefiore. In G. J. Biesta & D. Egea-Kuehne (Eds.), *Derrida & education* (pp. 176–185). Routledge.

Derrida, J. (2001). *On cosmopolitanism and forgiveness* (M. Dooley & M. Hughes, Trans.). Routledge. (Original work published 1997)

Edgoose, J. (2001). Just decide! Derrida and the ethical aporias of education. In G. J. Biesta & D. Egea-Kuehne (Eds.), *Derrida & education* (pp. 119–133). Routledge.

Fitzgerald, F. S. (1925). *The great Gatsby*. Scribner.

Foucault, M. (1990). *The History of Sexuality: Volume 1. An introduction* (R. Hurley, Trans.). Vintage. (Original work published 1978)

Grumet, M. (1988). *Bitter milk: Women and teaching*. University of Massachusetts Press.

Nord, W. A., & Haynes, C. C. (1998). *Taking religion seriously across the curriculum*. Association for Supervision and Curriculum Development.

Tell, D. (2007, November). Michel Foucault and the politics of confession. In *Annual meeting of the NCA 93rd Annual Convention, TBA, Chicago, IL* (Vol. 15).

ABOUT THE AUTHOR

HEIDI LYN HADLEY is an assistant professor and the director of the English Education program in the English department at Missouri State University. Her research interests include teacher education and identity, the intersection of religious and educational practice, and community and family literacy. She can be reached via email at hhadley@missouristate.edu.

INDEX